Christian Philosophy
and
Religious Renewal

Christian Philosophy

and

Religious Renewal

Edited by

George F. McLean, O.M.I.

78029

THE CATHOLIC UNIVERSITY OF AMERICA PRESS

Washington, D. C. 20017

Imprimi potest:

    William Ryan, O.M.I.
    Provincial

Nihil obstat:

    Patrick Aspell, O.M.I.
    Censor deputatus

Imprimatur:

    Patrick A. O'Boyle
    Archbishop of Washington

May 9, 1966

TABLE OF CONTENTS

ACKNOWLEDGMENTS

The editor wishes to acknowledge his gratitude to the distinguished authors of the separate studies included in this volume. To them, as to Sheed and Ward, Inc., for permission to quote from Karl Rahner's *Nature and Grace,* and to Miss Frances Margarelli and Mrs. Eleanore Walsh, who contributed generously to the preparation of the manuscript, he and this work remain truly indebted.

ACKNOWLEDGMENTS

FOREWORD

At the culmination of decades of religious ferment, the Second Vatican Council, as a historic convocation of the pastoral and teaching authority of the Church, constituted an eloquent proclamation of a religious renewal. Both the intention of the Council to "build a bridge toward the contemporary world" and the great interest in this project shown by all sectors of society testified that the roots of this question lay deep within the contemporary philosophy of man, his world, and his God. The studies in this volume examine the key notions and directive insights of this philosophy for their positive contributions in facing the challenge of renewal in a manner which will render possible a rich harvest of sound progress.

The investigation of the philosophical problem is carried out in three parts. The first states and evaluates the attempt to rediscover the sources of Christian philosophy in a phenomenology of Christian life. The second part analyzes the religious implications of the analytic and existential elements which must characterize any contemporary Christian philosophy. The third part studies the issues of person, freedom, love and ecumenism, isolating the philosophical elements involved and identifying the meaning of these insights for the realization of religious renewal. The presentation of the panel and round-table discussions follows as closely as possible the actual words of the discussants, although the material has been reorganized in order to facilitate a comparison of the views expressed and is presented as a report rather than as a transcript.

The highly integrated character of this series of studies is the fortunate result of their having been planned and executed as part of The Catholic University of America 75th anniversary philosophy workshop on "Christian Philosophy and Religious Renewal." The proceedings of that workshop have been published under the title *Christian Philosophy in the College and Seminary* (C.U.A., 1966) and contain reports on seminars concerning the content and teaching of a contemporary Christian philosophy, including one report of 130 pages on philosophy in the seminary, together with papers on the relation of philosophy to theology.

The present volume of studies contains a series of studies by the same editor concerning contemporary problems of philosophy and philosophers, and consisting of *Philosophy and the Integration of Contemporary Catholic Education* (1962), *Teaching Thomism Today* (1963), and *Philosophy in a Technological Culture* (1964). It is hoped that the publication of these studies will bring new insight concerning the challenges, as well as new hope for success in the urgent task of developing a Christian philosophy for the age of renewal.

GEORGE F. McLEAN, O.M.I.

The Catholic University of America
Washington, D. C.

PART I

CHRISTIAN PHENOMENOLOGY
and
THE CHRISTIAN PHILOSOPHER

PHENOMENOLOGY OF VALUES IN A
CHRISTIAN PHILOSOPHY

by

Dietrich von Hildebrand

The Crisis in Contemporary Moral Thought

A trend toward amorality can be observed in this epoch which must be clearly distinguished from immorality. It is a tendency to eliminate the moral point of view in man's approach to life. Whether one thinks of the relations between the two sexes, of a great part of contemporary literature, or of the attitude of many teachers in public colleges and high schools when dealing with history or literature, one encounters the attempt to oust the fundamental categories of morally good and evil and to interpret the world in an amoral approach. Instead of grasping the tremendous reality of the categories of morally good and evil and understanding them to have a function in the spiritual realm of human life similar to that of light and darkness in the exterior world, it is believed to be more objective and realistic to strip the world of its moral significance. It is not understood that in so doing one necessarily falsifies the nature of all the most important things, depriving them of their significance and capacity to bestow happiness on man. In a word, one reduces the world to a laboratory and condemns oneself to endless boredom.

Unfortunately the discrediting of morality is not restricted to these circles. Among Catholics, too, one can encounter a kind of blindness for the dignity, grandeur, and beauty of morality. Hence, it is possible to hear in a sermon that one has falsified the Gospel by stressing the importance of morality. Even the great and admirable French poet Paul Claudel has said: one will never succeed in making us love morality; we can only love Christ. Here the discrediting of morality and ethics assumes the character of opposing morality as a code of superimposed prohibitions to the splendor of the holiness of Christ.

It may well be asked: why this trend toward amorality; why this

3

defensiveness for morality? It is time to recognize that an insufficient presentation of morality in traditional ethics carries a heavy share of responsibility for this discrediting of morality outside and inside of the Catholic realm. This neutralized, humdrum, juridical presentation of morality has deprived it of all its existential power and breathtaking splendor. Very symptomatic of this failure is the revolt of situational and existential ethics, which we find in Catholic youth movements, and in writings of Mauriac, Graham Greene, and many others.

All this implies an imperative call for a rehabilitation of morality, an awakening to the all important fundamental significance of the categories of good and evil and to the splendor of moral values. A great responsibility weighs on Catholics to replace this dull and juridical presentation of ethics by an adequate one, which will do full justice to the inexhaustible wealth and depth of moral values which surrounds one in life, in Holy Scriptures, and in the lives of the saints. The task is to detect again the ultimate depth and significance of moral good and evil (of which the great Kierkegaard said: the ethical is the very breath of the eternal), and to present it not only to younger Catholic generations, but to the entire world.

Ethics and System

It is important to consider some fundamental problems in order to point out the reasons for this misrepresentation of ethics and the world of moral values. Some dangers arise from acting like Procrustes cutting the feet of people who did not fit in the bed he had made. Such a procedure is followed by those who are more eager to present a closed system than to do justice to reality, who believe that deduction is a more safe knowledge than is evident insight, and who refuse to admit a reality as long as they have not succeeded in explaining its relation to other truths. They forget Cardinal Newman's admirable words that ten thousand difficulties do not justify one single doubt and refuse to admit what Gabriel Marcel calls "the mysteries of being."

Moreover, when the ideas of a great philosopher have formed a school and taken on the character of a closed system that can be taught like a textbook, the members of such a school do not even do justice to the master whose disciples they claim to be. Because of the love for a system as such, they are led to overlook several important insights of the master which do not fit into this system.

A classical example for this is the discrepancy between Aristotelians and Aristotle himself. Each idea which is identified as pertaining to the closed system, although only cautiously presented by Aristotle, assumes a dogmatic character in the Arabic and Jewish Aristotelians; whereas those ideas in which Aristotle, forgetting his own theory, pierces through to a deeper level are more or less ignored. Which Aristotelian has noted that Aristotle,[1] in dealing with liberality, suddenly reaches a fundamental insight which revises his entire Mesotes theory?

> Now virtuous actions are noble and done for the sake of the noble. Therefore the liberal man, like other virtuous men, will give for the sake of the noble, and rightly; for he will give to the right people, the right amounts, and at the right time, with all the other qualifications that accompany right giving.

The Rehabilitation of Ethics

This rehabilitation of ethics emphatically has nothing to do with the unfortunate attempt to adapt traditional philosophy to modern systems and to strive for a concoction of Thomism with some Kantian, Hegelian, Heideggerian, or Freudian elements. It would rather revise traditional ethics by confronting it with reality: the world of moral data offered to us in life, in Holy Scripture, and in the saints. What is required is a rethinking of all the answers in ethics, and this will arise from a close contact with moral reality and with the plenitude of moral values and disvalues.

Such contact will make it possible to see that in many cases the truths grasped in traditional ethics call for further differentiation, for completion and enrichment. Above all, it will make evident the need for a *prise de conscience* of the many realities which are silently presupposed in the traditional philosophy, though not explicitly recognized and expressly admitted. In this reflection there would be appreciated the full philosophical meaning of a reality which is known in the immediate, living contact with reality. Such, for example, was Aristotle's appreciation of the four causes. This review also implies the elimination of all the tacit but never proven presuppositions which often bar the way to an adequate knowledge of the real nature of morality.

---

[1] *Nichomachean Ethics*, IV, c. 1, 1120 a 23-27.

Value Response

One might begin with the undeniable reality termed value response. When one considers one's attitude whether in responding to a moral call, in enthusing about a great work of art, or in many instances in the liturgy, he cannot but realize that in these situations he accomplishes a value response. This is a response to something because of its intrinsic importance, goodness, and beauty; a response in which one transcends the realm of his needs, desires, and appetites; a response whereby one is interested in something for its own sake.

For example one might ask concerning the words of the "Gloria": "Gratias agimus tibi, propter magnam gloriam tuam," or "Laudamus te, adoramus te" just what attitude these words embody? They clearly express that one not only thinks of God as one's supreme good, but that one responds to God's infinite holiness, glory, and goodness as such. One is fully aware that he owes this praise to God's infinite goodness. The words "quoniam tu solus sanctus, tu solus Dominus" plainly state that one's being is focused on God's intrinsic goodness, glory, holiness and beauty—on God as such.

In this there is presupposed all important and decisive datum of value, in contradistinction to the good for the person. What does one mean by the terms "holy" or "infinite goodness and beauty"? To which datum do these refer? Clearly they mean more than something beneficial for oneself, something which draws its importance from a relation to oneself or to other persons. They mean something which has its dignity and importance by its very nature and in itself.

In praising an action as morally good does one not univocally refer to something which is important in itself? In saying that a morally good action glorifies God, is it not referred to as a value with another type of importance than in the observation: "what a good for this man is his marriage or his good health or his creative talent"? These two types of importance are clearly distinguished, namely, the important in itself or value and the objective good for the person or the beneficial good. This is exemplified in hearing of a conversion when one rejoices about both the glorification of God which it implies and the good which this conversion also represents for the person in question. In thinking of the glorification of God, one's concern is with the value of the conversion; in referring to what it means for the convert, one's concern is with the beneficial good this conversion also represents.

This distinction is also to be found in the words of the Preface: "Dignum et justum est, aequum et salutare." The praise of God is first of all "dignum"; "justum et aequum" refer univocally to the value of the praise which is indissolubly linked to its oughtness. On the other hand, "salutare" refers to the fact that this praise of God is also a beneficial good for us.

In an existential approach to reality which, as Gabriel Marcel so aptly said, renders to experience its ontological weight, there is no possibility of overlooking the indisputable reality of value, to which one refers continually, which one presupposes inevitably, which belongs to the ultimate realities like being, truth, and knowledge, and to which one appeals even in the very same breath in which he attempts to deny them. The datum of value is presupposed in the philosophy of all epochs. But as oftentimes happens, the most indisputably and obviously presupposed realities are not expressly registered in a philosophical *prise de conscience* and only accidental hints at their existence can be found. Does not Aristotle clearly hint at the value, in contradistinction to the objective good, for the person when he asks: "Do men love, then, *the* good or what is good for *them?*"[2] Does he not refer clearly to value or the important in itself when, on many occasions, he calls one attitude more noble or Godlike than others?

Even one who would attempt to deny all morality, such as Aristippus of Cyrene for whom the only thing which matters is pleasure, presupposes tacitly the reality of value. He explains how one should pursue pleasure and opposes this way of acting by the "wise man" to the behaviour of the brute-like man.

Why would one reject the philosophical recognition of this tremendous reality which is also necessarily implied in the notion of God? Is the refusal to confront the datum of value justified by asking: what can these values be; what is their metaphysical place; or how can one prove their intrinsic importance? In the case of the beneficial good, because one can show that it is necessary for the existence of a person or that it serves his happiness, its importance is plausible. But in the case of a value, one cannot prove whence it derives its importance. Is one then entitled to deny a reality, which is so undeniably revealed to us that we cannot deny it with-

[2] *Ibid.*, VIII, c. 2, 1155 b 21.

out presupposing it simultaneously, because he has no answer for
all the problems it implies?

It belongs to the very nature of value to possess its importance in
itself. Thus the question whence it derives its importance is as
nonsensical as the questions: how do I know that something evident
is evident, or which criterion does one possess for evidence? In
reality the evidence of an importance in itself is much more intelligible, and this in a much deeper sense of the term intelligible,
than the plausibility offered by the notion of something being important for something else.

Furthermore, the datum of value offers not the slightest contradiction to traditional philosophy. It reflects the normal process
of a further differentiation of the notion of bonum and an appreciation of something which traditional philosophy continually presupposed without, however, registering it philosophically. "Developing an idea suggested by St. Anslem, Scotus points out that
in man there is a second, more noble affection or inclination, the
affectio justitiae. This is a tendency or inclination to appreciate
what is good and perfect for its own sake, to take complacency in
what is fine and beautiful even where this has no relation to oneself." (Father Wolter)

Value and Morality

Unless one understands moral goodness in its character as a value
and moral evil as a disvalue, one can never reach or illustrate the
impact of the morally good and evil. As long as one ignores the
value response, one can never do justice to the transcendence of the
person, to its deepest feature as an imago Dei. One must not identify
morality with the immanent striving for self-perfection or with
reasonable behaviour. Instead, one must clearly distinguish from
the necessity to conform to the neutral immanent laws of all things
in order to attain one's goal, the categorical obligation to conform
to the moral law, the call issuing from morally relevant values.
Otherwise, one can never do justice to the impact of morality, its
oughtness, its unique relation with our eternal end, the ultimate
seriousness of the moral question transcending our earthly existence,
or the mysterium iniquitatis of moral wickedness.

As long as one remains in the realm of hypothetical, neutral, immanent laws to which one must conform in order to attain his end,
he would be acting as one would with the laws of mechanics if he

wanted to construct a machine, with the laws of logic and grammar if he wanted to write a book, or with the physiological laws of the human body if he wanted to preserve his health. Instead one must turn to the completely different laws expressed in the Decalogue, such as "thou shalt not kill," with their completely different atmosphere, their axiological impact, their breath of the eternal, their absoluteness, and their definitely anti-neutral character. Only then can one understand the nature of sin and the tremendous disharmony which it creates as an offense to God.

As long as one ignores the existence of morally relevant values and disvalues and remains on the mere question of choosing adequate means for attaining a certain end, he creates an unbridgeable abyss between the doctrine of original sin as a moral evil and all its tremendous consequences. Can there be imagined a greater stress on the impact of morality than the doctrine of the expiation of the offense created through original sin by the God-man's death on the Cross?

Yet it is not enough to admit the reality of values which cannot be reduced to the beneficial good or the objective good of the person. One must also recognize the difference between two fundamental categories of motivation: the merely subjectively satisfying and the value motivation. It is precisely here that the entire moral drama of man displays itself, for here lies the source of moral wrong. This consists in ignoring the call issuing from a morally relevant good because one allows himself to be determined exclusively from the point of view of that which is subjectively satisfying for him.

It is wrong to believe that it is only the choice of means which separates actions that are morally good from those that are evil. In reality the difference comes from the two radically different points of view mentioned above for basing one's motivation in approaching the world. The difference can be clearly grasped if one compares the determining point of view in the motivation of an Aristippus of Cyrene with that of a Socrates. It is the same fundamental difference in the direction of will which St. Augustine emphasizes in his *De Civitate Dei* when he wrote that there is a will directed to God and one directed to oneself.

The failure to admit the reality of values and the failure to understand the value response in which one is motivated precisely by the point of view of the value, has also led many to some confusion concerning the morally good and the merely morally unobjectionable. Instead of trying to elaborate the positive value of purity, meekness, justice, generosity and humility, in all their splendor, beauty, depth and oughtness, one has been content to emphasize the question of the morally unobjectionable. Both the morally objectionable and the positive moral value have been called morally good. Important as is the question of whether or not something is morally unobjectionable, still the difference between the merely morally unobjectionable and the positive moral goodness is of the utmost importance. Indeed, it is precisely in focussing on the positive moral goodness that the beauty and glory of morality can be thrown into relief.

Natural and Supernatural

Another prejudice barring the way from presenting morality in all its depth, height and breadth, is the conviction that philosophical ethics must abstain from mentioning the plenitude of moral data found in the saints or, as it might be put, the Christian virtues characteristic of the new creature in Christ. One erroneously believes that, because these virtues presuppose faith, they belong exclusively to moral theology. This prejudice is based on a confusion of two completely different facts. One fact is that these virtues are fruits of the Holy Ghost and presuppose sanctifying grace. Now this certainly belongs to theology and not to philosophy, for it can be known only through revelation and is not accessible to a natural experience. But a completely different fact is the appearing reality of the Christian virtues themselves. The extraordinary quality of Christian morality, the new ethics witnessed in the saints, their likeness to Christ, their humility, their charity, all these are data which can be grasped in experience, and which are definitely not something which are possessed only in faith.

A still further confusion is responsible for banishing the analysis of this supernatural morality for ethics. It is true that these virtues presuppose the Judeo-Christian revelation as object in order to come to pass. A man can only be humble if he believes in the God of the Bible, insofar as this is a response to the God revealed in the Old and New Testaments; the morality of the saints presupposes the Christian faith. But, once these virtues have become a reality, the philosopher does not need faith in order to grasp the extraordinary quality and moral value of charity, humility, or mercifulness.

Thus it is very understandable that Aristotle did not know the virtue of humility, because he never was confronted with this reality. Aristotle praises pride—not the ridiculous vanity, pretentiousness, or overrating of one's virtues and perfections which is based on error and lack of objectivity—but the pride which is based on great achievements, heroic deeds, and virtues. It is not because Aristotle did not himself possess the Christian faith that he did not see the moral value of humility, but because he never had the opportunity to see it in another person.

Bergson, on the contrary, though not possessing himself the Christian faith, clearly grasped the extraordinary moral value in the life of a St. Teresa of Avila. Because these virtues had become a reality in the Christian realm, he had the opportunity to grasp their embodiment in historical figures. This purely philosophical insight led him to consider this morality as the higher and authentic one.

I often wonder that one has considered angelology to be a valid topic of philosophy. I myself would not dare to philosophize about angels because, unfortunately, I have not had the privilege of experiencing a close contact with my guardian angel, like a St. Francisca of Rome. One knows angels through revelation alone. But the saints are an historical reality; their morality is manifest in their deeds and words, and still more in their entire personality. It is thus a pure prejudice to exclude them artificially from ethics.

One who is not blind cannot but see the qualitative difference between the noble morality of a Socrates and the sublime, transfigured morality of a St. Paul or a St. Francis of Assisi. All this can be done without presupposing faith or referring to revelation. It is a task proper to an authentic ethics to analyze this supernatural morality in order to show both that it infinitely surpasses all natural morality as something completely new, and simultaneously that it is the fulfillment and crowning of all natural morality. In supernatural morality every moral attitude assumes a new quality by the fact that it is a response to Christ and to the world seen in the light of Christ. All morality becomes a manifestation of the love of God and every concrete value response is consciously linked to God, the sum and source of all values. None of this can be seen if one is grasped by the prejudice that philosophical ethics is restricted to natural morality. This prejudice must share the blame for the watering down of morality and for its presentation in a way which discredits it. The ousting of the Christian morality from philosophical ethics deprives morality of its incomparably higher part, while the failure to show the intrinsic relation of natural morality to Christian morality makes of ethics a mere code of reasonable behaviour.

Affective Life and Morality

Another disastrous prejudice is the exclusion of the entire affective life from the spiritual part of man. This unfortunate heritage from Greek intellectualism has never been really proven and is still less evident. Here again one is confronted with an unfortunate abstractionism which cuts itself off from the plenitude of being. Instead of opening the eyes of the mind and consulting reality, it takes an arbitrary assumption for granted and interprets reality according to that assumption. If one considers without prejudice affective value responses such as joy over the conversion of a sinner or deep contrition over a sin, one cannot but state that they possess all the meaningful features and intelligibility which characterize a theoretical response such as the conviction of a truth evidently grasped or an act of will conforming to the moral appeal.

This prejudice has had disastrous consequences. It has created false difficulties, false alternatives, and false interpretations of most fundamental realities. As a result, in order to save its spiritual character, love has been deprived of its affective character and made either an act of will, an appetite striving for self-perfection, or even a mere movement towards an end. The central place granted to love and charity in the Gospel made it obviously impossible to abandon love and especially charity to the non-spiritual part in man. Thus, as one accepted the verdict of the non-spirituality of all affective experiences, the artificial problem imposed itself of interpreting love as something non-affective and as an act of will. The observation of St. Paul that if one did not have charity he would still be nothing, though he gave all his goods to the poor, definitely excludes such an interpretation of love. Since good will is obviously present in the desire to give all one's possessions to the poor, love must be more than an act of will.

An abyss yawns between one's experience and existential approach to certain affective responses on the one hand, and on the other the philosophical treatment of these affective responses. The same man who is deeply moved when witnessing an heroic and glorious love or a true contrition, such as the tears of Peter after his denial of Jesus, as soon as he reflects upon these higher types of affectivity will declare that feelings do not matter and have no real value. This is a typical case of an unwillingness to reconsider in the light of reality the thesis concerning the non-spiritual character of all affectivity.

Affectivity and Spirit

If one approached reality unprejudiced, one would see that it is indispensable to distinguish between radically different levels in the realm of affectivity, just as one must distinguish between radically different levels in the sphere of intellect. Many experiences such as moods, bad humor, depression, and jolliness after drinking an alcoholic beverage have a definitely non-spiritual character. But these types of affective experiences differ as much from such an affective value response as joy over the conversion of a sinner or deep contrition, as a meaningless and quasi mechanical association differs from a luminous insight.

It is a grave error to overlook these essentially different levels in the realm of affectivity and deny the spirituality of some affective value responses. It is also quite inadequate to subsume these affective value responses under the notion of passions and then point to the non-spiritual character of passions in order to deny the spirituality of these affective value responses.

In mediaeval philosophy, terms were used in a very wide or analogous sense. In this way the term will was used for all types of meaningful responses without distinguishing between volitional and affective responses. Even in interpreting love as an act of will one did not expressly strip love of its affective character. Today, however, the term will is existentially understood in its precise sense as the remarkable act which is at the basis of all actions and whose object is not yet real, though realizable through me. This volitional response clearly differs from affective responses such as joy, admiration, veneration and love. Hence, though in theory one may maintain the term will in the analogous sense in which it extends to these affective responses, in fact he replaces it tacitly by the univocal sense.

Thus, today when a preacher says in a sermon: in the love of one's neighbor what matters is not what you feel, but exclusively what you will, he refers to the will in the precise sense, and really denies all value to the affective value response of love. This is a typical example of the necessity of new differentiations and distinctions which, far from contradicting former insights, would complete them and make them more adequate and precise.

It is time to realize that affectivity and spirituality are not incompatible to do justice in an unprejudiced analysis to the nature of these fully affective and highly spiritual experiences. If one examines the nature of an affective value response, such as the joy over the conversion of a sinner or the freeing of an unjustly imprisoned man, one must see that this response of one's heart has the same meaningful response character as a response of one's intellect. In both cases, an act of knowledge is presupposed. It is necessary to know the fact that someone has been converted or released from prison in order to rejoice over it, just as it is necessary first to grasp a fact in order to be convinced of its existence. Yet one must not only know the fact, he must understand its significance and grasp its value in order to rejoice over it. All these presupposed acts are definitely spiritual and highly rational.

Furthermore, the joy itself has the character of a meaningful response, of a conscious and intelligible relation to the object. To use this term in the sense of Husserl, it is an intentional act. Unlike any psychic state, such as bad humor, which is merely caused and which is perfectly experienced even when we have no knowledge of the cause, joy necessarily presupposes one's knowledge of the object motivating it. It possesses a conscious meaningful relation to its object; it aims at this object and means it. Yet in this affective value response of joy, one finds even more significant marks of its spiritual character over and above its meaningful, intentional response character.

This joy also possesses a character of transcendence, a meaningful conforming to the value of the object. It transcends the entire realm of immanence, of the unfolding of appetites, urges, desires, and passions; it shares with knowledge the conforming to the nature of the object. Just as in grasping an object one does not appease an appetite but transcends oneself in conforming to the object, so one transcends himself here in his interest for this good for its own sake. If knowledge is an "adequatio intellectus ad rem," what happens in an affective value response can be characterized as an "adequatio cordis ad valorem." The same mark of transcendence is to be found here as in knowledge or in a conviction based on evident knowledge. This transcendence is one of the fundamental marks of a spiritual attitude; it is strictly opposed to all experiences which belong more or less to the biological sphere and depend upon our body.

Hand in hand with the denial of the spirituality of affectivity goes the thesis that affectivity essentially presupposes the body and is linked to it in a completely different way than is any act of knowledge or of willing. However, this thesis is by no means evident, nor has it been ever really proven. In fact, this prejudice flows again from the mistake of using the lowest type of affective experience as the pattern for affectivity as such.

In reality there are several types of feeling which essentially presuppose the body, but this does not apply at all to the higher types of affectivity. A headache or the pain felt when one is wounded are bodily feelings in the strict sense of the word. In these cases the feelings are clearly voices of the body, dealing with the body, and mostly located in the body. Yet certain affective experiences, which in themselves differ radically from the above mentioned bodily feelings, can also depend upon the body. States of depression, bad humor, or unrest are indeed not bodily experiences, but they are linked to the body in manifold ways. Even though their nature does not make them a voice of the body, they still may be caused by mere physiological processes.

The above is not the case with affective value responses. A value responding joy, or love, or veneration presupposes the body not a whit more than an act of will or of knowledge. There is, of course, the general mysterious relation between the soul and body, but acts of will and of intellect are no more exempt of this mysterious relation than are affective responses. The fact that they have bodily repercussions which thinking or willing do not have, does not entitle one to claim that these responses depend upon the body. The fact that a spiritual act is so powerful that it has repercussions upon the body implies rather the very opposite of a dependence upon the body. In this connection, one need only think of mystical ecstasies which, in spite of their effects on the body, will never for that reason be considered non-spiritual.

These hints may suffice to prove that prejudices alone can lead to a denial of the spirituality of affective value response, and to the assumption of an alleged incompatibility between affectivity or the heart and spirituality.

It must not be forgotten that in speaking of happiness, one inevitably refers to an affective experience rather than to an intellectual or volitional one. Happiness which is not felt is a contradictory notion, just as is a decision which is not willed, a theory which is not thought, a color which is only heard, or a tone which is only seen. It is a striking contradiction for Aristotle to declare happiness to be the ultimate end and simultaneously deny the existence of a spiritual affectivity. Even if he were right in claiming that knowledge is the highest source of happiness, happiness itself must always be felt. Instead of denying the existence of spiritual affectivity, one should rather insist on the differences in the affective sphere, clearly distinguishing the spiritual from the non-spiritual type of affectivity and clarifying the precise nature of the feeling at stake in the experience of that most sublime happiness which corresponds to beatitude.

It is time to tear down the walls separating philosophy from the plenitude of life and to do justice to the all important role of affectivity, of the heart, in human life as well as in the Gospel and liturgy. How can one expect to understand the Cross, the unfathomable depth of the passion of our Lord, or Gethsemane, if affectivity is thought of and presented as something secondary, belonging to the non-spiritual part of man? Traditional philosophy's downgrading of affectivity is incompatible with the role assigned to the highest affective experiences in the Gospel. Do not the words of our Lord: "My soul is sad unto death" pierce one's heart in their ineffable sublimity; or is this piercing of one's heart not an equally affective and deeply spiritual experience?

Phenomenology

Finally it is necessary to find one's way out of the dead alley into which the ousting of all affectivity from the spiritual part of man has placed philosophy. Freed from this prejudice, one must elaborate the depth and sublimity which only affective spirituality can display. How insufficient and tainted with an unreal abstractionism is, for instance, the philosophy of love when compared with the inexhaustible richness and depth of this glorious reality in all its different types and categories! To do justice to this reality one must start with the personal act of love, not with vague analogies to appetites and motions which can be found also in the impersonal realm. One must start with the datum at stake when a friend loves another, a mother loves her child, or a husband loves his wife. One must begin with the specific personal act which is meant in speaking of love, whereby it is clearly distinguished from other positive affective responses such as enthusiasm, admiration, or esteem. This concreteness and immediate contact with life must not be understood as a mere empirical description or psychological observation. Instead, one must approach this datum and focus on its intelligible essence in the specifically philosophic attitude which I call phenomenology.

This term has assumed many different meanings, especially in Husserl's teaching after 1913. The sense in which the term is used here differs radically from the one found in Father Lauer's *Triumph of Subjectivity*.[3] Here phenomenology refers to the immediate intuitive contact with the intelligible data of experience and to the analysis of their essences, in contradistinction to all kinds of exploration of their genesis, hypotheses, or abstract explanatory constructions. It is the method used by all great philosophers of the past in their discoveries and insights, whether we think of the *Organon* of Aristotle, the distinction between the four causes in the first book of his *Metaphysics*, St. Augustine's discovery of the true nature of free will in his *De Libero Arbitrio*, Kant's distinction between analytic and synthetic judgments, or his distinction between categorical and hypothetical obligations. All this has been grasped by an intuitive analysis of the given or by strict deductions, whereas many other statements of the philosophers are constructions and hypotheses.

Humility

The above may be illustrated in the case of the concrete virtue of humility, concerning which further differentiation and deepening of the traditional ethics vital for the rehabilitation of morality should be undertaken. Simultaneously, this example may serve to illustrate the method of phenomenology in the sense of the term in which it is synonymous with the classical philosophical mode of procedure by which all decisive philosophical insights were attained.

Instead of starting from the four cardinal virtues and asking under which of these four it can be subsumed, one should delve

3 (New York: Fordham Univ. Press, 1958.)

into the parable of the pharisee and the publican. Why take for granted that the cardinal virtues really cover the entire field of morality? Why approach the analysis of humility with this preoccupation of fitting it into one of these cardinal virtues? One might thereby jeopardize from the beginning an unprejudiced attempt to delve into the nature of this virtue and grasp its specific quality and characteristic features unhindered by any other preoccupation.

The first task which imposes itself is to distinguish humility from the other apparently allied virtue of modesty, in the sense of unpretentiousness rather than of chastity. A modest man in this sense does not overrate his capacities, is able to recognize that another man is superior to him, and is ready to admit this superiority without any bitterness. Modesty in this sense is also opposed to vanity and arrogance. It is a lovable virtue; but it clearly differs from humility, with its overwhelming depth and beauty. Modesty is a virtue which does not presuppose the knowledge of God and still less a lived confrontation with a personal God, whereas humility necessarily implies this confrontation. Therefore modesty has a specifically friendly flavor, whereas humility has an ultimate impact. Modesty belongs to the sphere of natural virtues, such as justice, which can be practiced by pagans.

A further typical difference is that in modesty there is an element of resignation, a retiring in the background. In true humility there is not the slightest resignation, but a joyful, blissful admission of unworthiness and nothingness. The modest man sees the reason for his unpretentiousness in the fact that his intelligence or the stature of his personality is inferior to that of others. For the humble man, on the contrary, the question of his achievements, virtues, and perfections plays no role in the motivation of his humility. His is the blissful admission that whatever may be positive in him is simply a gift of God, and that measured by what he could be in cooperating more with the grace of God he is only a useless servant.

In modesty, pride is only overcome to the point of enabling the man both to be objective rather than blind to his limitations and inferiority with respect to others, and to admit this openly and without grudge. In humility, however, there is not only an incomparably more radical victory over pride and a capacity to recognize objectively one's limitations and even admit without grudge the superiority of others. There is even a holy paradox:

the higher a value ranks with which one is endowed, the more will the humble man abstain from glorifying himself in it. The less stupid it would be to feel superior, the more humility forbids it. To be proud about a moustache is certainly more stupid than to be proud because of a great artistic gift, but the latter pride is much worse. When it comes to moral virtues, for which the human person is more responsible than for the artistic talent which is obviously a pure gift, to glory in them is not only a much more fatal type of pride but even destroys and dissolves the moral virtues.

Humility is the highest and most important of all virtues apart from charity. It is the one which is most emphasized by Christ apart from charity and which makes even the sinner lovable. One can only hint at the revolution taking place in the parable of the pharisee and the publican, at the breath of eternity and the ultimate freedom implied in humility. Without any reference to grace or to revelation as object of faith, one must detect the role which faith plays in humility which is possible only as a response to the God of Christian revelation.

It is obviously impossible here to enumerate all those features of humility which are immediately disclosed by the phenomenological approach. Even all these features would only be a modest beginning when measured by the unfathomable depth of this virtue. It is, however, especially important to stress the unique relation which this virtue has to the entire morality of a person, just as its opposite, pride, invalidates all other virtues. The same cannot be said of justice, purity, or generosity.

Again the inner link between contrition and humility must be elaborated. Every true contrition implies a breakthrough of humility, a breaking down of the walls of the fortress of our pride, a surrender. The humble man cannot but recognize his sinfulness and repent for it.

Finally, when all is said, it must be recognized that in humility there dwells an element of mystery and a holy, blissful freedom which puts to shame all mere reasonability. It presupposes confrontation with God and, for its full blossoming, the consciousness of being sheltered in the infinite love of God.

THE CHRISTIAN PHILOSOPHER

by

GERMAIN G. GRISEZ

It would be a mistake to consider only what Christian philosophy is. It makes sense to ask what elephants are or what elements are; but Christian philosophy is not that sort of entity. Its reality is not a mere fact; instead its very nature depends upon norms and man's consideration. If one is captivated by historicism, it seems natural to talk as if Christian philosophy were a thing existing independently. The important, but forgotten, distinction between nature and culture would underline the fact that Christian philosophy does not have the status of an object of purely speculative knowledge. It is not among those things which reason cannot make but only considers. Christian philosophy is not there like a carbon atom or an oak tree or a rainbow; the objectivity of the past is only memory, not reality.

Christian philosophy by its very nature depends upon man's consideration. One is a Christian and a philosopher; he is so by choice, in fact by two choices. Hence, the real question is: what is one to be as a Christian and as a philosopher; how is one to knit together this life?

Christian Philosophy as History

Maritain's widely accepted view is summarized in the statement that Christianity belongs not to the definition of philosophy but to its concrete reality. This statement means that "Christian" is predicated of philosophy only *per accidens*. Philosophy as such is not and cannot be Christian. The next question is how philosophy happens to be qualified by what it is not essentially. To answer this question, one must use history as a speculative discipline and set out on a long investigation into the unreality of the past, trying to discern intelligibility in the *per accidens* where there is none. But why should one be concerned about what Christian philosophy was? Simply as a matter of past fact it is of no great account, and purely speculative history is particularly useless and unpleasant.

20

The Christian Use of Philosophy

If, however, one attends to the real point at issue, the view changes drastically. The real issue is what road Christian philosophers are going to take. For each individually, the question is what is meant by his vocation to be a Christian philosopher. By what responsibilities and fulfillments is it defined? For all together, the question is what the direction of the philosophic community will be.

If one begins to look at philosophy in this practical way there is one distinction which is absolutely essential. This stands between, on the one hand, philosophy in its own right: the philosophical activity, work, and life of the philosopher as such; and, on the other hand, philosophy functioning as an instrument: philosophy being used by something that is not philosophy.

The use of a philosophy, particularly of a metaphysics, usually means its destruction. The only exception is the case in which faith as supernatural makes good use of philosophy. Christianity can make use of philosophy without destroying, deforming, or ruining it; but this is only a possibility.

It is a fact, and one by which Catholic philosophers need not be embarrassed, that almost all the philosophy taught in Catholic institutions—in seminaries, teachers' colleges, sister-formation movements, and colleges for lay students—is not philosophy pure and simple. It is philosophy being used as an instrument. I do not say there is anything wrong with this situation, but there is a danger that such Christian philosophy, like "religious art," might degenerate. Christian philosophy, in the sense of philosophy utilized as an instrument of Christianity, can degenerate very easily into what is found in manuals. It can become intellectually vacuous, boringly repetitious, and out of all contact with experience. Such decadent scholasticism has no real meaning or value.

To discover a solution to this problem one must bear in mind that philosophy used as an instrument is in dialogue, that is, it is in a human situation to which there are two sides. The student need neither be a philosopher, become a philosopher, nor receive philosophy itself. With few exceptions, it does not seem to me necessary, for example, that those who have a vocation to the priesthood should become philosophers or should understand philosophy in itself. I doubt that there should be any philosophy, properly so called, in the seminary curriculum.

Yet philosophy must be used in the seminary curriculum, because the Catholic faith is contained in a tradition, which, whether one likes it or not, has been heavily influenced by philosophy. Although one need not be a philosopher, if he has none of the things that only philosophy can provide, he will have a very difficult time making sense of Catholic doctrine. Thus philosophy must be used as an instrument. What is more, those who are involved in this use—those teaching in the seminary, planning the curriculum, or writing the books—should be real philosophers. To have good liturgical art, each pastor need not be an artist, but he should hire somebody who is a real artist rather than a "religious artist." Those charged with staffing a seminary or with making appointments to the faculty of a Catholic college should be sure they have real philosophers.

Discrimination of the genuine is very difficult here as it is with regard to art. But the fact that a distinction is subtle does not mean that it is unimportant or able to be ignored without bad consequences. A subtle distinction must be constantly kept in mind and constantly respected.

Augustinianism and Thomism

Some might consider it an insult to call a philosopher an Augustinian and an essentialist; but Augustine is a great saint, a father and doctor of the Church. Dr. von Hildebrand, it would seem, is an Augustinian. He insists upon clarification, stresses the affective side, and demands constant contact with experience; his rhetorical style even has a certain touch of Augustinianism about it. Even when Dr. von Hildebrand talked favorably about system, it was fairly clear that the exemplar for the system he would accept could only be a work such as Augustine's *De Trinitate*. This masterpiece is systematic in a certain sense, but it certainly is not a system formed by the canons of the *Posterior Analytics*. The Augustinian tradition is a great one in Christian philosophy and in Dr. von Hildebrand's work one finds an example of how alive, wholesome, and sound it can be today, and how very much in contact with what is of value in contemporary thought. Clearly all can profit very much from this work.

On the other hand, Father Ashley thinks basically as a Thomist. Of course, he also wants clarification in order to understand what things are. But he wants something more than that: he is primarily interested in explanation, in the knitting together of facts in causal accounts. Even when Father Ashley worked as a phenomenologist, he was still Aristotelian in selecting a definite problem, analyzing it, and responding to it very neatly and beautifully. In speaking well about existentialism, his comments still had the methodological structure taught in the *Posterior Analytics*.

There are here two distinct meanings of "Christian philosophy," two great modes of thought in Christian tradition. There is no need to discard either of these because the difference between them is not one of irreconcilable opposition, but rather a matter of what is deemed important and emphasized. Such differences do not necessarily lead to conflicts or generate issues; the Augustinian and Thomistic approaches can live very comfortably side by side. Thus, there are at least two senses of "Christian philosophy."

Augustine on Nature and Grace

If one conceives philosophy as an attempt to answer the question: how can I live a good life, then philosophy is reduced to ethics or even to prudential judgment. If so, then there can be only three kinds of answers to such questions as: how can one be happy? One kind of answer is reasonable but unsatisfying, because unworkable in practice. A second kind of answer is unreasonable but more satisfying. Such, for example, are the answers proposed by the primitive cultures: they can be put into practice, but demand a great deal of suppression of reason for a fairly well functioning society. The third kind of answer to the moral question is offered by Christianity. It can be satisfying because it can be both reasonable and lived. If one who begins from ethical questions demands that practicability of ethics that is required if the ethics is to be complete, it is inevitable that he end by transcending pure philosophy and entering the realm of faith. The phenomenon of the restless heart, upon which Augustine fastened, is connected with this difficulty. It consists in the fact that such natural goods as truth, justice, and friendship, for which man reasonably strives and which he should be able to attain by his natural ability, are unobtainable by fallen man. Once man is fallen, unless assisted by grace, his performances are always short of his resolutions. To deny this is to deny the doctrine of original sin of which Augustine was so conscious.

What is not obvious is that the experience of failure to achieve what one wishes makes one radically dissatisfied with the natural end which should be a satisfying life for a reasonable man. Reasonably moderated efforts with fair success would not leave one discontented and the restless heart would not occur. But, in fact, one's efforts are not thus moderated and they inevitably fail.

Augustine did not know that the restlessness he experienced is not universal. Discontent can be avoided if a solution is accepted that involves a certain amount of irrationality. The primitives and many eastern cultures have accepted such solutions, and contemporary western secular humanism also is attempting to establish a solution which carefully delimits the domain in which reason is permitted to operate. Hence restlessness is not inevitable, but only occurs when reason becomes dominant in a culture and makes its full set of demands. Since they cannot be fulfilled, one must either become a Christian or be doomed to be unhappy. That was Augustine's experience.

Speaking naturally, there is no real reason to suppose that man should attain perfect happiness. Yet when one finds his reasonable desires frustrated, he conceives and wishes for perfect happiness. A reasonable person would not wish naturally for what is beyond his grasp; but with revelation he accepts in faith and hope that grace will make perfect happiness supernaturally possible for him. As a result he easily confuses the notion that man by nature is entitled to be perfectly happy with the truth that God by virtue of supernatural gifts has made man to rest in Himself. One thinks that this should be naturally true because he is frustrated with what naturally should satisfy him.

Now if fallen nature were healed without being elevated, man's existential dilemma would be solved just as effectively. In that case he would not desire what he has no right to expect and could achieve all that he reasonably desires. Nature has no exigency for grace except insofar as fallen nature requires to be healed.

Unfortunately, Augustine himself was by no means clear about this distinction between healing grace and elevating grace. How could he be, for he had not well distinguished between nature and grace. Hence he was led to identify man's experienced dissatisfaction with a desire for God, when in fact the natural desire is only a frustrated wish for what is strictly due nature and which, as frustrated, easily leads man to form an irrational desire for perfection. Thus when Augustine comes to look at philosophy, he cannot imagine it ever being satisfactory in itself. Philosophy always must be transcended, and the philosophy that is transcended is always more or less erroneous. The critique of philosophical errors, Augustine thinks, leads man to transphilosophical truths.

Dr. von Hildebrand's position is Augustinian, but with a difference. He does not try to undo history since Augustine's time in order to take a stand with him, but takes into account the distinction between nature and grace as Augustine never clearly did. Thus Dr. von Hildebrand insists upon the claim of philosophical knowledge to a certain absolute validity. It is the truth itself that counts and he very definitely, clearly, and completely rejects fideism which would allow philosophy to be relativized for the sake of exalting faith.

A second evidence of the character of Dr. von Hildebrand's Augustinianism appears when he urges that one must take into account the phenomena of the Christian saints and describe their virtues. In urging this he notes that it is one thing to look at these phenomenologically and another thing to consider them in the light of faith, concluding that to consider them in the light of faith transcends philosophy. This makes a clear distinction which one does not find in Augustine for whom faith and reason are joined together or, really, not yet adequately distinguished.

Thus in Dr. von Hildebrand's work one finds an Augustinianism that has become sophisticated by incorporating the development of theology in which the distinction between nature and grace has been clarified. There is here no relativism in the form of a fideism which would hold that philosophy can never really lead to anything without faith.

Nature and Grace Confused

However, there is another kind of Augustinianism which fails to make these distinctions. It accepts the potential alternative, inherent in Augustine's confusion, that implies relativism or fideism with respect to natural knowledge and claims that philosophy is really worthless until transformed by faith. This view is not in any genuine sense a Christian philosophy, for a Christian should not accept it. He can see in the light of faith that it is not necessary to reconcile the errors of fallen nature with the truths of redeemed nature.

The proper philosophy for a Christian should be the work of nature healed and already redeemed, not the work of fallen nature;

though, of course, redemption is incomplete and still in process. Pure philosophy is possible only for a Christian, because if one is not a Christian he is affected, whether he realizes it or not, by the alternative to Christianity—fallen and unredeemed nature. If one does not accept faith, he somehow rejects it with a distorting effect. Only if one accepts Christian truth is it possible, though not necessary, for the distinctions required for pure philosophy to be made.

Those who confuse faith and reason should not be considered more Christian as philosophers than those who insist upon distinguishing them. That the confusion of the two is considered more relevant to contemporary problems could be due to a desire on the part of contemporary man not for philosophy but for easy answers, quick satisfaction, or support for a weak faith which becomes nervous unless it finds bolstering from reason.

During the Middle Ages gradual progress was made toward removing the confusion between principles in Augustine. In this the biggest step was made by Thomas Aquinas who clarified the alternative between the assertion of the distinction of faith and reason as compatible with Catholic faith and the denial of this distinction as incompatible with faith.

Aquinas did not think of nature and grace as if they were two layers or compartments. To think of them in that way assumes that they are generically the same and differentiated within what is fundamentally the same schema or single whole. Aquinas never said that grace and nature interpenetrate. This currently popular image is as dangerous as any other, because grace and nature can interpenetrate only if both share characteristics as do objects in a single genus.

Grace and nature for Aquinas are infinitely more diverse than two species of single genus; they are analogous to one another. Grace and nature are so diverse that no level image, or compartment image, or interpenetration image can do justice to their relationship. There can be no third thing within man by which the two are united; the principle of unity between grace and nature lies only in God who is the author and the end of both.

Of course, the Christian is both natural and graced. But to look for a link or a dividing line between the two in man is absurd. Everything about man is natural; and if a man has grace, everything about him is graced. Anything which can be observed, discerned, or understood in a man, be he Christian or not, is natural. The liturgy of the Eucharist, insofar as it is a visible rite capable of being observed and understood from the observation, is natural. That does not mean that it is not supernatural, for the two are not contrary to one another.

Everything human which man in the state of fallen, redeemed, or integral nature has done is natural. Everything in man is natural; but everything in Christian man—the whole man—is also graced. Even the curl in the saint's beard is graced and just as truly as his freedom is graced, though of course the two are not equally important.

It is an error to think that grace and nature are two moments, aspects, or elements in a single human existence, for this is to relate the two realities of nature and grace to the one abstraction, human existence. Nature and grace are real; human existence is an abstraction. This abstraction either directly vitiates both nature and grace or does so indirectly by subtly reducing one to the other.

Aquinas himself did not see all the implications of his own principles, but after the Reformation, when the Church faced the challenge of widespread confusion about nature and grace, she had the work of Aquinas to use as a starting point for her clarification. The great scholastic theologians went very far toward making this clarification, although their work was not always perfect. The lesser scholastics and the textbook presentations of theology were even less perfect, as popularization always occurs at some cost to truth. Nevertheless, the chief results of the post-Reformation development in the doctrine of grace belong to the essence of Catholic tradition. One cannot go back.

Recent Problems on Nature and Grace

How, then, should one proceed? Obviously, it is our task to make the distinction all the more precise and complete. Only by distinguishing nature and grace completely and removing from our notion of either anything truly characteristic of the other can one come to understand, in the sense that the human mind can understand, the mysterious duality in which God has chosen to create and to re-create man. The implication of such theological progress for Christian life is that grace could be more perfectly understood to transform nature without at all tending to interfere with it, alter it, or suppress it. That grace heals nature is not interference.

This road toward theological progress has not been followed by many during the last twenty years. There has, instead, been a great deal of nostalgia for past ages of theology. Many theologians fear forward movement and are eager to return to the Church fathers, apparently as a way of escaping issues which a Christian's faith and reason should face in our time. Their "new theology" is an out-moded antiquarianism. Unfortunately theology is not an innocent hobby, and more unfortunate still, popular fashions in theology do not follow the most solid work and profit from the effects of the most acute criticism.

In current theology, especially in fashionable popular works, the distinction between nature and grace is completely confused through the identification of the supernatural with the existential. This confusion is found in Father Henri de Lubac's *Surnaturel*. "Spiritual" has come to be used ambiguously to refer either to all that pertains to the human person and subject or to what peculiar-ly pertains to the life of divine grace. Many completely confuse these two, opposing both of them to the natural.

The word "nature" is either treated with disdain or diluted until it is nearly meaningless. However, the existential, personal, and subjective are just as truly natural and distinct from the super-natural as are the anatomical and the physiological. Freedom is as natural as is the curl in one's beard.

From this there results a distinction between two kinds of Augustinianism, resulting from an ambiguity in Augustine himself. One kind of Augustinianism has taken into account subsequent clarification of the distinction between nature and grace, and hence would seem to be fully acceptable. The other kind of Augustinian-ism falls into the error of confusing nature and grace after they have been distinguished in the more developed doctrine of the later tradition, and such fixated Augustinianism would seem to be quite unacceptable.

The Christian Philosopher

In view of the above, it is now possible to ask what should be accepted as the responsibility and expected as the reward of one's vocation as a Christian philosopher? What should be the direction of the philosophic community; with whom should it cooperate and whom should it oppose in its professional work? Obviously, based on a respect for nature, a great deal will be demanded for philosophy.

There is a sense in which the Christian philosopher is in the same position as the Christian mathematician, the Christian politician, and the Christian baseball player. This sense usually is quickly set aside in discussions of Christian philosophy as if it were not very significant. Nevertheless this is the most important sense in which one can be a Christian philosopher. Rather than excluding the others, it includes them; hence it is the basic sense because it indicates the one thing that is always necessary.

Just because the term "Christian philosopher" in this sense is the least definite in specification and the least interesting from the point of view of speculative history, its meaning has the greatest importance. "Christian philosopher" in this sense indicates what can be the result only of the conjunction of grace and nature, while the other senses indicate what can be the result of uninformed faith or of delusion. All other senses of "Christian philosopher" have counterparts signifying factors that are natural and that affect philosophy as if they were simple alternatives to Christianity or other modes of human life that one might adopt if he did not happen to be a Christian. This basic sense of "Christian philosopher" has no positive alternative in nature itself.

If one were a Christian and a baseball player, how would he determine what his proper life should be? It would be to play baseball to the best of his ability and at the same time to live as a Christian to the best of his ability. The problem is one of simultaneity, not one of history. History really has little to do with human reality. Time is a factor in human life; but it is one of the less important ones.

There are at least three ways in which one could achieve integration if one were a Christian baseball player. First, one could consider baseball a worthwhile activity in itself. One would want to take part in it because it comes forth from God, like all good things. To the extent that one is a Christian he would want to play better baseball, because he would be more interested in baseball and less interested in himself. Dr. von Hildebrand has noted this above where he discussed intrinsic value.

In the second place, baseball is a Christlike activity which requires the use of intelligence and freedom, spirit, muscle, and skill. It is Christlike, simply because it is human. Since to the extent that one is a Christian he would want to be as Christlike as possible, he would try to play better baseball.

In the third place, if one loved God as a Christian, one would want to achieve whatever good he could as a better imitation of His perfection. One's baseball playing would be the stuff, the real content, of one's Christian life. Therefore one would do it and place it on the altar at the offertory to be transformed in Christ. This sacrifice of baseball on the altar would imply that it was played with charitable love for one's family, teammates, and, not least, spectators. One would want to entertain them, because charity had led one into the world to make an irreplaceable contribution to human good, and this particular good would be what one would have to share with others.

Perhaps some baseball players have approached this Christian ideal. Unfortunately, philosophers are subject to somewhat more temptations in their professional lives than are baseball players. They should simply be doing philosophy to the hilt. It is not their business as philosophers to explicate the faith or to devote themselves to the concerns of theology, though if philosophy helps theology so much the better.

The primary business of the philosopher is speculative truth, not the happy life. Although ethics is an important philosophic concern, it should remain a subordinate one. The sense of "Christian philosophy" which admits of a pure metaphysics is superior to the sense which basically restricts philosophy to the ethical. Truth is not exclusively theoretical, but it is primarily so.

Personalism

There is a strong trend observable in Catholic philosophy today toward a type of personalism or degenerate existentialism (as Dr. von Hildebrand observed in his "Dangers in Constructing a Contemporary Christian Philosophy," in *Christian Philosophy in the College and Seminary*, ed. George F. McLean, O.M.I. [Washington: The Catholic Univ. of America Press, 1966]), and which presupposes the unacceptable mode of Augustinianism. Metaphysics is said to be a study of man and being, or of being in relation to man. This division of the subject of metaphysics establishes man as part of its primary and specifying object. There is no problem if ethics is the main concern of a certain philosopher, so long as he does not reject the right of metaphysics to a position beyond ethics, though such a philosopher simply is not a metaphysician. But there is a major problem if ethics is substituted for metaphysics, for then man is constituted the center of all things.

If the subject matter of metaphysics is man and being, then man is exempted from his proper place within being. Rather than being considered where he belongs within being, he is set apart as a special principle and thus becomes the subject for metaphysics insofar as he is divided against the rest of being. The presuppositions underlying this view are subjectivistic. Once based on this ground a metaphysics can never be built straight and true.

This approach cannot escape all the Kantian problems. In truth, the only real principle divided against the being metaphysics studies is God. To take as the primary and specifying subject matter of metaphysics both man and being is implicitly to confuse, however remotely, man with God. God alone remains outside the being metaphysics studies as its principle. Man is a principle of truth, but he is included in, rather than constituting a transcendent principle of, the being studied by metaphysics.

If "man," that is consciousness or subjectivity, is set over against being from the outset, then to be knowing and to be real necessarily appear as incompatible, and reality must be characterized as what always transcends subjectivity. Consciousness becomes a negation or gap. Consequently, since it is impossible that in God reality and consciousness should be perfectly identified, God, as an impossible ideal, cannot exist. In this way Sartre consistently works out the position that starts from man and being.

The truth in existentialism can be saved in a more adequate metaphysics, which does justice to all the orders of being without distorting everything by unduly exalting human subjectivity. Christian ethics can learn from existentialism, just as it has learned from phenomenology. But Christian ethics is only a secondary concern of philosophy and cannot be allowed to become the primary concern, without losing the humility man's place in reality requires. In that case it would become a mixture of bad philosophy and good faith, for since only Christianity offers a reasonable and satisfying answer to man's most self-centered questions, ethics hardly can exist without eventually calling on faith.

Some turn to existential philosophy as superior to naturalism in its treatment of the problems of metaphysics and theology, though both naturalism and existentialism are reductionisms merely using different devices and reducing to diverse modes of entity. Certainly, one has trouble if he imagines God to cause free acts in the same way that a natural cause causes a natural effect; but one also has trouble if he imagines God to cause free acts in the same way that one person causes the free acts of another. Persuasion is as little the way that God causes free acts as is a physical push and the fact that persuasion is more personal than the push does not mean it is more like the divine causality of human action. Divine causality altogether transcends both modes of finite causality, and difficulties will be encountered equally whichever of these it erroneously is thought to be.

Others turn to existential philosophy in order to avoid abstractions and deal with the concrete and with real life. This concrete-abstract distinction is used constantly today as a rhetorical device. An unwanted position is called a partial view, a mere abstraction, "all right in theory, but not reality." There are endless opportunities to do this because to perceive is to abstract, to think is to abstract, and to be other than God is to be abstract. The standard of the concrete is the all-perfect. Any dialectician can easily apply this standard to one's ideas and so condemn them as merely abstract.

Hegel was expert in the use of this device and it is now used by all the dialecticians among the anti-Hegelians: pragmatists, dialectical materialists, and existentialists. It should be noticed that the accuser's concrete also is abstract, and often in a less intelligible and more emotional way. The scholastic saying: to abstract is not to lie, is founded on the fact that not-to-be-God is not the same as to-be-nothing. Finite reality is not unreality and partial falsehood, despite what Hegel says. In fact, anyone who would agree with Hegel must simply be substituting his own version of truth, which is a different partial truth, for divine truth.

The Contemporary Task of the Christian Philosopher

One's responsibility as a philosopher is to reality and to truth. The philosopher must be a constant critic of what is fashionable because all movements oscillate irrationally between extremes. This is as true of movements in the Church as it is of any others. When liberalism is strong, it is the task of the philosophers to defend the conservative values. When conservatism is dominant, it is his task to defend the liberal values. When legalism is dominant in morality, he should stress personal values and freedom. But when situationism begins to appear, he should defend objective values including such material goods as human life and the procreative good which is an essential and irreducible human value.

Only reason can moderate the irrational swings of the movement between an absurd legalism and a pseudo-mystical personalism. It is the most solemn obligation of the Christian philosopher to try to inject some reason. Because he seeks to follow reason it will forever be necessary for the Christian philosopher, in accord with the mind of the Church, to oppose the popular trend in the Church.

This responsibility is no less serious during a time of Christian renewal when there is increased hope for Christian reunion. One's actual faith, hope, and charity are somewhat imperfect and to this degree can mislead one as well as guide him aright. The ecumenical movement seems to be unqualifiedly good and is naturally close to all hearts. Still if one's actual charity is not perfect but mixed with a certain amount of selfishness, then even here this heart can lead one astray.

One subtle way to be selfish, especially common among Americans, is to want to be liked and to get along well with everyone in an affable and relaxed fashion. Pleasant personal relations are easily mistaken for charity and relationships purportedly grounded in love can involve exploitation which is hidden or disguised. True and perfect charity could never trespass upon the rights of nature or of reason, but imperfect charity which is sentimental and accompanied by rationalization easily can trample over their claims.

Thus the chief present task of Christian philosophers is to remain at their post, defending both nature and reason. The principle of subsidiarity applies here; each sphere should have its own distinct and responsible authority and subordinate spheres should not concern themselves with the problems of the whole. Philosophy can help Christian renewal best by doing its own work well. It is the duty of philosophy to guard theologians, the pastorally oriented bishops, as well as the Christian community at large against an excessive enthusiasm which easily produces a willingness to surrender rational consistency and such merely natural goods as the initiation of human life.

Far from impeding the ecumenical movement, labor at the philosopher's proper task will be of great assistance. Such labor can steer the movement away from many blind paths into which it otherwise might turn and from which it would only have to return again. The Holy Spirit never will sanction a Christian unity based upon the violation of reason or of natural goods. God has made us rational animals and undoubtedly wants us to behave accordingly, as did the Incarnate Word of God Himself.

How is one to integrate his complex vocation of being simultaneously a pure philosopher and a Catholic Christian? The advice of Leo XIII is to start from those in tradition who best achieved integration in the fulfillment of their office; in particular, he proposed Thomas Aquinas as a model. It would not be in accord with Leo's advice and the disciplinary intent of the Church to use copious quotations from Aquinas to illustrate thinking that originated elsewhere. What is meant is rather to begin from Aquinas and to depart from him precisely as far as evidence and reason demand. Each philosopher must ultimately judge these demands, using his sources of evidence and his reason. He cannot avoid final responsibility for his own judgment, because he has no philosophic superior.

Philosophic argument is not a strategy of proselytizing. Genuine philosophy must criticize other philosophy and offer itself to all other philosophy for criticism. This exchange is not a dialogue; it is a bloody conflict without which philosophy would not progress. To reject unlimited critique is to reject philosophy and manifest oneself interested only in talking with those who share a special jargon or accept a special set of presuppositions which are not to be criticized.

The chief task of the Christian philosopher is to bring his best efforts, his grace assisted and hope comforted efforts, to bear upon current philosophical problems. For most of us this should mean the problems of concern to English-speaking philosophers. Problems engaging continental thinkers should be a secondary concern for us, because we are less likely to contribute effectively to the work to be done on them, while the work that waits here certainly is not going to be done by Catholic philosophers in Germany, France, or Italy.

In sum, the Christian philosopher's primary aim should be to do the work of speculative philosophy—first philosophy, pure metaphysics—and this work can and should be done as pure philosophy. A secondary, but by no means incidental concern, should be the work of ethics. Ethics cannot remain pure philosophy if it becomes concerned with moral dynamics, with the achievement of the good life. Pure philosophy can tell us what a good human life should be, but it cannot provide effective guidance, since one does not do that which he would.

Christianity is not merely a religion, a supramoral solution to man's existential problem. Primarily, Christianity is the inroad of God upon creation. The inroad is called Christ and all the effects of God in creation are connected with the Incarnation. Christianity also is a meaningful revelation received by man through and in symbols, especially linguistic ones. Finally, Christianity is the use of all things in the worship of God.

This Christian use of all things in the worship of God sacramentalizes creation in a way that essentially transcends the merely religious. Nature of itself could not achieve such a thing; but redeemed nature with grace will achieve it. The Christian attitude demands unqualified respect for all natural values, because every instrument must first have its own action. Man is to be saved only because he is part of a whole creation which is to be supernaturalized. All the rest of creation is for the perfection of rational creatures only because they are the best parts of a universe whose all-inclusive order is the very best of created realities. That one's own beatitude should reflect divine goodness is more important than that it should fulfill one's desires, though the two are in no way opposed.

Consequently, it is important to recognize and respect immanent, natural, non-moral, and non-personal values. What is most important is not one's salvation, but the divine goodness. Therefore, the value inherent in the procreative good or in speculative truth must be loved in such a way that one would no more directly violate them than he would directly violate mutual love or Christian reunion.

In times past philosophy was given a large place in the curriculum of Catholic colleges because it was thought necessary for ethics and theology, or because it was thought to be good apologetics, or because the college philosophy curriculum was adapted from the seminary program. Now philosophy should keep an important place in the college curriculum because of a recognition of its inherent value. Philosophy should be loved for its own sake by every Christian, even if it butters no bread, makes no dialogue, or offers no help to ecumenism. Philosophy belongs to the perfection of the kingdom of God, for that kingdom is secular too, and all things, including pure speculation, must be restored to God through Christ.

PART II

CONTEMPORARY COMPONENTS
OF CHRISTIAN PHILOSOPHY

ANALYTIC PHILOSOPHY AND LANGUAGE ABOUT GOD

by

REVEREND W. NORRIS CLARKE, S.J.

In studying the relation of contemporary philosophical movements to religious renewal, in the spirit of *aggiornamento* of Popes
John and Paul and the Second Vatican Council, it seems a little
strange to reflect upon analytic philosophy. Surely there could
hardly be two more opposite poles than the coolly detached, impersonal attitude of contemporary analytic philosophy and the warm-
ly personal, committed attitude of religion. Yet it has always been
the case that every significant movement in philosophy has influenced Christian thought and through it Christian religious attitudes. In the present case it can be genuinely fruitful both for
Christian philosophy and religious renewal to meet the challenge
of this particular contemporary philosophical movement.

The reason is this. Man's knowledge of God is always a delicate,
even a precarious balance; it is an inner tension between knowing
and unknowing, between the positive and the negative. The best
that even positive knowledge can do is to point toward a God
hidden in mystery, without ever grasping or understanding Him
clearly in finite concepts. As St. Thomas keeps insisting, in phrases
that never cease partially to scandalize some: "The essence of God,
what God is, is totally unknown to us."[1] But whenever man has
moved forward, through the efforts of some great thinker like
St. Thomas, to a new level of precision in the positive knowledge of
God, as time goes on he tends to settle down comfortably. He begins
to lose the awareness of the precariousness and tension within his
finite knowledge of the Infinite; in a word, he begins to think that
he knows more about God than he actually does. This seems
inevitable as the hard-won achievement of one thinker turns into
the traditional doctrine of a school which, after a while, requires
more effort to question than to accept.

It is here that one can note the beneficial role of challenge from

[1] See *Summa Theologica*, I, q. 3, a. 4, ad 2m; *Summa contra Gentiles*, I, c. 30
and III, c. 49.

the outside. If it is met squarely, it often shakes up too easily held certitudes and makes one rethink freshly and creatively the whole problem. This very effort plunges one back into that austere but fruitful semi-darkness in which it becomes necessary to reach out again anxiously with one's mind in order to reconquer or rediscover that in which one's human knowledge of God, with its vital tension between knowing and unknowing, darkness and light, really consists. It is in just such an existential atmosphere of personal intellectual and volitional reaching out towards the hidden God that the religious attitude of faith can experience a fresh and vital renewal.

Something like this can happen from the confrontation between, on the one hand, the traditionally accepted philosophical and religious knowledge of God and, on the other, what at first sight appears to be a dangerously threatening challenge to the meaningfulness of this knowledge from contemporary logical and linguistic analysis. The following will sketch in broad lines both that in which this challenge consists and the way in which it can contribute to a renewal of Christian philosophy. The breadth of the strokes required to give a composite picture will imply some lack of nuance and inevitable oversimplification of issues.

Analytic Philosophy: A General Description

The particular concern in this paper is with the school of "ordinary language" or "linguistic analysis" philosophy, which forms part of the general current of analytic philosophy that has developed within the last twenty-five years. The aim which generally characterizes this movement is, not to construct philosophical explanations or systems of its own, but rather to analyze precisely the meaning and logical propriety of already existing language: whether this be the language of science, or of philosophy, or of theology, or simply the philosophically relevant categories of ordinary everyday language. We might for convenience divide the movement into three main streams, though each overlaps the other at not a few points.[2]

Logical Empiricism. The first branch of the movement is logical

[2] An introductory bibliography will be found at the end of this article. Most of the items contain bibliographical indications for the particular topics. In the succeeding notes we will refer to items on the bibliography by number only, e.g., #1.

positivism, often known as logical empiricism since it adds modern logical techniques to the old empiricism.[3] It stems from the Vienna Circle group founded just before World War II by Schlick, Carnap, and others. This school, for all its logical and empirical claims, turned out to be in fact a doctrinaire or a priori anti-metaphysical position, based on the famous verification principle of meaning. According to this theory, a concept or proposition had meaning only if it could be verified or reduced in some way to publicly verifiable sense experience. This, of course, dispensed in principle with any discussion of non-observable entities like God, the soul, the intellect, or any metaphysical principles which by their nature are inaccessible to sense experience.

The extremism of this particular school quickly came under fire for arbitrariness from all sides, so that it has been forced into a steady retreat from its original claims. Historians objected that the past was robbed of all proper meaning, since it was reduced to mean nothing other than the present evidence for propositions containing verbs in the past tense. Scientists objected that highly theoretical conceptual constructs and hypotheses indispensable to contemporary science but not directly verifiable in experiments were rendered meaningless. Philosophers objected that the very verification principle of meaning itself, being a universal negative, could never be verified in any experience or set of experiences: hence, the highly embarrassing consequence that the verification principle was itself meaningless. As a result, logical positivists had to withdraw their assertion of the verification principle of meaning as a truth. It was reduced to the status of a rule, which is neither true nor false, but a freely adopted way of achieving an end. Hence, it cannot be imposed on someone unless he wants to achieve this given end and no other means is possible—questions, obviously, which cannot be settled by invoking the rule itself.

The doctrine in its characteristic original form has now been abandoned by all save a few. One finds scarcely any philosopher on the American or British scene who is now willing to call himself a logical positivist. Its quasi-official laying to rest was presided over recently by one of the best known spokesmen for the movement, Herbert Feigl of the University of Minnesota, in his highly significant—and charmingly frank—Presidential Address for the Western Division of the American Philosophical Association for 1962-63,

[3] #1-3 in bibliography.

in which he reviewed his whole career as a philosopher and re-counted the steps of his gradual withdrawal from logical positivism.[4] Nevertheless, it is important to recognize that its spirit is still very much alive in various more subtle forms and, as will be noted below, indirectly influences not a few thinkers.

Symbolic Logic and Semantics. The second main branch of the movement is composed of the various branches of technical analytic philosophy, strongest in this country, but existing also in the Scandinavian countries, Switzerland, Holland, Italy, and elsewhere. This comprises the schools of symbolic logic and semantics, prin-cipally those interested in constructing precise artificial languages for more rigorous logical and conceptual analysis of the language of science and allied fields. This group will not be of direct con-cern here either, since it has not to any notable extent applied its techniques to the analysis of philosophical or religious language about God.

Linguistic Analysis. The group which is here of direct concern is the third, often called the "ordinary language" school or "linguistic analysis" philosophy.[5] It objects to being considered as one single school, committed to a fixed body of identical doctrines. Originat-ing in England with G. E. Moore and still the dominant philosophy there, this general stream or orientation is not interested in con-structing new artificial languages. Rather, it analyzes the precise meaning of the basic categories of ordinary language and applies them to other areas of discourse or "language games," such as philosophy, theology, law, and to a certain extent even science. It considers the ordinary or everyday language of a people to be the fundamental matrix from which all other more specialized and artificially constructed modes of language take birth and to which recourse must be had to explain their meanings and rules. In par-ticular, ordinary language is also the ultimate, at least negative, regulative norm or court of appeal for checking the meaningfulness and relevance of all philosophical language.

The central operative insight which gave birth to this movement and still sustains its development was the discovery that at least some traditional philosophical problems or hotly controverted positions are not the result of any problems forced upon one by reality itself. Instead they arise from language confusion or muddles,

4 H. Feigl, "The Power of Positivistic Thinking," *Proceedings of the American Philosophical Association,* XXXVI (1962-1963), 21-42.
5 See #1, 3, 4, 5, 6, 10, 12, 14.

stemming from "category mistakes" or the misuse of terms distorted from their natural context in ordinary language. In these cases some term has been taken out of the ordinary language context in which it is "at home" and applied in some new context. In the process the term has been twisted into at least a partially new meaning, yet holding on to enough of the old meaning to give the impression that it is still the same term or concept that is being discussed. The result is that the new use of the old term conceals within it several disparate or incompatible meanings, often jumbling several different categories into one. This produces a language muddle or category mistake, which can breed endless false and insoluble problems.

The worst of it is that the philosopher in question either does not realize what he has done most of the time and hence cannot get out of his difficulty by himself (like a fly in a bottle, says Wittgenstein) or, if he does realize it, keeps playing on the double meaning of his term in order to keep his problem or novel position going. Because philosophers in the past have not been aware of what they are doing linguistically, they have raised pseudo-problems of all sorts. These remain insoluble because the very language in which they were formulated contains hidden category confusions or even nonsense propositions, as though one were to ask, "How fast can numbers run?" or "What color are sentences?" Obviously no answer is possible to such questions because they are meaningless from the start.

Because the language muddles of philosophers are more subtle and hard to detect than the above examples they need special "therapy." Thus to ask, "Is perhaps my whole life just a dream or illusion?" involves a linguistic muddle, even though it sounds like a deep and difficult problem. The ordinary language use of the term 'dreaming' is to describe certain particular types of experience which are distinguished from others called 'waking.' It is by nature a contrast word, deriving its meaning from contrast with a meaningful opposite. Therefore, to ask whether the totality of my experiences might consist in dreaming would be to destroy the contrasting correlative of 'dreaming' and thus rob 'dreaming' itself of any specifiable meaning. If the suggested hypothesis were true, the term 'dreaming' would never have existed in its present meaning at all or would at once lose its standard meaning.

Similarly, to ask "What is time?" is to make a category mistake.

In ordinary language 'time' is used in sentences like: "What time is it?" or "How much time does this take?" But one does not say, "What is time?" One asks "What is a cabbage?" or "What is a gnu?" because these are thing or substance words. But 'time' does not function like a thing word at all. For the philosopher to try and make it function as such, as he does when he asks "What is time?", is to confuse two different linguistic and conceptual categories. It produces a muddled question to which no clear answer can be given. Similar analyses could be made of questions like: "Is space or time real?", or "Can time be speeded up or does it flow at a steady pace?"

When confronted with the contention of certain idealists that "Time is unreal," one of G. E. Moore's favorite refutations was to ask, "Oh, you mean that I didn't eat my lunch after my breakfast, that I ate my lunch at the same time that I ate my breakfast?" If the philosopher protested this was not what he meant, Moore would answer that if he did not mean this then he had changed the ordinary meaning of 'time' without indicating what the new meaning was.

The initial insight was quite sound in observing that some philosophical problems either conceal or have arisen as a result of language muddles by using a term native to one context or category in another and incompatible one without warning of a change of meaning. From this original modest position of G. E. Moore himself, linguistic analysts drifted rapidly toward the position that most, if not all, philosophical problems result from language muddles. Hence, they can be "solved," or rather dissolved, by the careful analysis of the meaning of the term used which would restore them to the original living "language game" or native habitat from which they had been lifted.

This general linguistic analysis school can be divided roughly into two main branches, one *negative* and the other *positive*. The first works on the premise that *all* philosophical problems are cases of linguistic muddles or pseudo-problems. The work of the linguistic analysis "philosopher" is therefore one of linguistic "therapy": to dissolve these muddles as they arise, and then to stop. He would have nothing positive to say on his own. Thus when, if ever, he has completed this task, he will have eliminated philosophy itself. This current stems from Wittgenstein in the second phase of his *Philosophical Investigations,* after the repudiation of the

Tractatus. It was for a while, perhaps, the dominant trend in this extreme negative form, but has slowly become more moderate and tends now to blend a good deal with the more positive current.

The positive branch, which is now more widespread, has a primary positive aim in addition to the above indispensable role of negative therapy. Its intent is to map out by positive analysis the authentic meaning of the main categories of ordinary language, so that whatever real problems remain in philosophy can be worked on without confusion and with a better chance of attaining whatever solutions are possible. At least it will be possible to understand clearly what is meant by the great basic categories or types of terms used in ordinary language. The same techniques can in principle be applied to any living language game, such as the law, science, and according to some even religious language. This program of negative therapy plus positive elucidation of living language is today certainly the dominant trend in linguistic analysis both in England and elsewhere.

By way of personal evaluation, it might be added that as long as one does not reduce philosophy exclusively to linguistic analysis, there are very valuable contributions which can be made both by the negative and positive techniques of this approach. Much purification and clarification of philosophical thought and language can result if philosophers constantly check up on themselves by asking: What do I really mean when I make this statement or assert this position? Am I merely changing the language or making a proposal for language revision when I put forward this position; or am I really expressing a new truth? Does my position render meaningless or inconsistent any basic category of ordinary language such as statements of motion, space or time, consciousness, or personal responsibility?

It has now become clear that Aristotle and St. Thomas both made far more extensive and effective use of such techniques than has till recently been suspected. Thus Aristotle refutes the Megaric position that nothing is possible save what is actual by showing that this would render meaningless the basic language categories of habit, skill, and capacity, in such a way that when a musician is not actually playing one would have to say not "He can play the harp," but rather "He cannot do so." St. Thomas puts forward as one of his main arguments against plurality of substantial forms in man that it would render invalid the essential predication "Man

is an animal." Since one does in fact speak this way quite meaningfully, any theory which destroys the meaning of such a predication
must quite rightly be considered ipso facto false for him without
any further argument needed.[6]

The negative techniques are also peculiarly effective in dissolving
by purely internal analysis any all-out reductionist theory of
reality, such as, "Everything is material," "Everything is living," or
"All my experience is a dream." If such terms as 'material' and
'living' which were made up as restrictive contrast words to distinguish one kind of being from another now include all possible
types of being, either it becomes impossible to say just what they
do mean or they become doctrines expressing a mere hope for the
future. Thus if 'material' does not mean physico-chemical as we
now know it but also includes human consciousness, which we
cannot yet reduce to physico-chemical laws, then 'material' means
simply 'whatever is,' or 'one hopes some day to reduce it all to
physico-chemical laws like those now known.' Even then it is not
clear what meaning the last phrases can have. The more sophisticated position, however, that everything is inseparable from
physico-chemical operations is not susceptible to the same easy
dissolution.

Application to Language about God

Both of these linguistic analysis groups have turned their attention in recent years with special intensity to what is certainly the
most challenging, puzzling, and problem-laden area of human language: language about God, both religious and philosophical. One
of the reasons why they found this field peculiarly apt for their
type of analysis is the fact that almost all the terms used to speak of
God, such as cause, personal, knowing, good, and provident, are
drawn from ordinary language. Yet it is precisely here that the
resources of human language are strained to the utmost in the
attempt to express through these words a domain beyond human
experience.

The results of this application of linguistic analysis to language
about God have been partly negative and partly positive. The
negative ones have been, if not the majority, at least the best known

---

[6] See #11 for a challenging account of how closely the results of constructive
analysis parallel the conclusions of metaphysicians like Aristotle, though in
different terminology.

and the most discussed. They are also the most challenging, and therefore the most stimulating to the renewal of our philosophical, theological, and religious thinking about God. Hence, what follows will concentrate principally upon them.[7]

Impossibility of Proving the Existence of God. The first challenge of linguistic analysis to traditional thinking about God has to do with the possibility of proving the existence of God philosophically. On this point ordinary language analysis joins with practically all the schools of analytic philosophy and with most schools of contemporary philosophy in agreeing that it is impossible to give anything like a formal proof of the existence of God. In particular, it declares all the traditional proofs either positively invalid or simply not rigorous proofs in any acceptable modern sense of the term.[8]

This widespread agreement among contemporary philosophical schools seems worthy of reflection. It is true that many of the particular objections against the traditional metaphysical proofs are themselves commanded by explicit or implicit metaphysical attitudes drawn from classical modern philosophers like Hume and Kant, or from the more or less hidden postulates of logical positivism. These can be ignored here, since they are hardy perennials already well known. More significant is the general reason behind all these denials, namely, that the notion of proof is understood in a much more rigorous and formal way today than in the past. This is the result of the intense cultivation of logic and semantics in our day, with its development of keener logical tools and a greater sensitivity to the hidden postulates which lie behind various types of arguments.

Thus the argument from effect to cause and especially to a transcendent cause of a higher order is the heart of practically all traditional proofs for the existence of God from Aristotle on. Nevertheless, it would not be considered by most modern philosophers, even theists, as a proof capable of formulation in rigorous formal logical terms and reducible to the basic logical principles of contradiction and excluded middle. The reason for this is that it presupposes the distinct postulate, irreducible to contradiction, of the principle of sufficient reason or the intelligibility of being. This, in turn, must be given the status, not of a logically analytic propo-

7 See #1 and 15 to the end; especially, as samples of negative critique, #19, 20, 22, 25, 27.
8 See #16-18, 23.

sition, but of a primitive postulate or synthetic a priori which is impervious to any further logical reduction. It posits the ultimate a priori of a primordial harmony and correlation of mind with reality, of the intellectual order and its exigencies with the ontological order.

This implies the assertion, which includes in one vast exceptionless sweep the whole of being, that nothing whatsoever that would be positively and radically unintelligible—such as, for example, a being coming into existence without any cause—can possibly exist in the real order. The immediate corollary of this principle is that if one finds any being or aspect of a being which by itself alone would clearly show itself to be unintelligible, then somewhere else in being there is a sufficient reason for this being in need. This latter is what is called a cause, and every being lacking the sufficient reason for its own existence must have another real being as cause.

Now it is quite true that as soon as one begins to exercise his intellect in order to understand and explain reality and to solve real problems, he is in fact, at least implicitly, using or living this principle. It would be impossible to carry on the life of the intelligence without accepting it in practice. Furthermore, every successful use of it in a particular case goes to build up an endlessly growing partial confirmation.

What the contemporary analysis of proof has made it possible to realize more clearly is that the assertion of the principle of sufficient reason or intelligibility in all its unqualified universality is not as transparently self-evident a truth as the principle of contradiction, which finite created minds can grasp in such a way as to be able to dominate it fully and see clearly here and now why it is and must be the case. To attain this clarity concerning the principle of intelligibility one would have to be the primordial identity of both being and intelligence and the ultimate source and correlator of all beings and intellects, that is, God himself. It is not possible to prove this principle by appeal to any other truth, since all explanation and all proof that is not purely formal and reducible to the principle of contradiction presupposes it.

This evidently rejects as a *petitio principii* all attempts by modern scholastics (the ancients had the good sense never to attempt such a thing) to reduce the principle of sufficient reason or causality to that of contradiction. It is indeed unintelligible to assert that something can come into existence completely out of nothing with no cause at all. Still this is in no way a logical contradiction or reducible to one, since it never asserts that being is nothing or that nothing is being. The principle of contradiction is static, like all logic; the principle of sufficient reason and its immediate corollary of causality are dynamic, like all existential explanation.

The finite intelligence of man is here brought up against the experience, which is highly fruitful both philosophically and religiously, of being plunged into the awe-inspiring mystery of its own finitude. It is the inescapable exigency that man must somehow humbly accept his nature and in particular the nature of his intellect as a given, a gift, somehow efficaciously pre-oriented and adapted to a conscious luminous possession of an order of being that, correlatively, is also simultaneously pre-adapted to intellectual possession by human consciousness. Thus, at the roots of man's entire intellectual life there is uncovered a radical act of what might be called natural faith, in the sense of commitment to what cannot fully be seen and justified without residue by one's own powers, in response to a mysterious summons or invitation issuing from the depths of the innate natural dynamism of one's created intelligence.

Only in terms of this radical act of natural faith in one's own human nature as a gift to be accepted can one, through reason and philosophy, make the leap of intelligence to God, or in fact the explanatory leap from any existential effect to its unperceived cause. All proofs of God are ultimately reducible to this: "If being is intelligible, then God is. But being is intelligible. Therefore God is." The minor is inseparable from the basic existential option, commitment, and risk outlined above. This option is an eminently reasonable one—in fact the only reasonable one—to make. But because it is not a purely formal logical necessity and not yet a total vision, it still involves an element of commitment beyond vision, and hence of risk.

The ancients for the most part, and especially the medievals, made this commitment spontaneously and naturally, being content to leave it implicit or take it for granted as outside of philosophical discussion. Perhaps the latter were not fully aware of how far their existentially prior commitment to Christian revelation predisposed them powerfully towards this logically prior act of natural faith in their own intelligences. Modern man, pitilessly self-conscious and living in a pluralistic world of belief and unbelief, can no longer take this underlying act of faith for granted. He must bring it out into the open and make his commitment or rejection of it fully explicit and self-conscious. He must be fully aware of the existential risk involved in living the life of intelligence at all and in freely accepting the responsibility for its assumption.

Thus, by a strangely ironical paradox, contemporary analytic philosophy, with its coolly impersonal methods of logical analysis, joins hands with its apparent opposites, continental existentialism and personalism. Both challenge the pretensions of nineteenth-century rationalism, including its manifestations within Catholic philosophy itself. This contemporary assessment of the limited role and efficacy of strict rational proof in the life of the mind is one of the most potent and pervasive influences of contemporary philosophy on current religious attitudes, among Catholics as well as others. The end of the age of rationalism in Catholic philosophy and theology has been widely heralded.

This sheds a new light on the old problem of the relations between faith and reason. It points to the fact that, without some pre-philosophical commitment of faith to an ultimate Source and Correlator of both finite being and human intelligence, it may be too difficult for self-doubting modern man to make the humble natural act of faith in his own finite intelligence as a given to be accepted. Without this he cannot help but fall into scepticism, even with regard to this-worldly achievements of his own mind. May it indeed be necessary, as Anselm insisted, that I must believe in order that I may understand?

Meaninglessness of Language about God. It is time now to proceed to some of the more particular challenges of the linguistic analysts to the validity of language about God. In general these challenges stem from the claim that language about God is by the nature of the case either incorrigibly confused or else positively meaningless. It may indeed express sincere emotional attitudes and perhaps specifically unique religious feelings, but it cannot suffice to express meaningful objective assertions about something or someone in the real order.

The fundamental reason is always the same. Religious or philosophical language about God is built up by borrowing terms from some other field or established human discourse, principally that of ordinary human experience. These are then transposed with a new twist in meaning to express something totally beyond and different from the area of experience which the terms were originally made up to express, and in which any understanding of their meaning must always remain imbedded. The old meaning no longer strictly applies, and there is no way of specifying the new meaning in terms of any common experience, since the new entity is by definition beyond all human experience. To attempt to construct new meanings in this way with no new experience in which to ground them or by which to test them is to attempt to fly without wings or to think in a vacuum; it can lead only to confusion, vacuousness, or downright nonsense. It should be carefully noted that in this approach it is not a question of proving propositions about God to be false, but simply of dismissing them as semantic nonsense or doubletalk.

Is 'God' a Name or a Description? Let us take a brief look first at one technical objection of this sort. It maintains that the term 'God' as used in religious and much philosophical language is an inextricable confusion of two quite distinct and irreducible linguistic and conceptual categories: proper names and descriptions. A proper name, like 'John,' designates a singular individual but does not describe him; it has reference but no meaning. On the other hand, a description or descriptive term, like 'man,' 'the Creator of the universe,' or 'an infinite being' signifies a meaning, but does not itself designate any referent or bearer of the description. In fact, it is quite possible that none exists. Thus one can ask, "Is there an infinite being, or a dinosaur?" and answer quite meaningfully—whether truly or falsely is another question—"No, there is not." A name points out some actual bearer, but does not describe it. A description expresses a meaning, but neither points out any actual bearer nor even asserts that there is one. The two kinds of terms function quite differently; they have a different logical grammar.

Turning to language about God, especially religious language, one discovers that the term 'God' functions simultaneously or in quick alternation as both name and description. Thus 'God' is used just like 'John' to designate and actually address in invocation that concrete being whom one believes to be the Creator of the universe. The proof is that it is used without any article: one does not say 'a God' or 'the God,' like 'a man,' or 'the Creator of the universe' and one addresses Him in prayer, "O God, help me," exactly as "O Mary, help us." Yet in other uses, sometimes within the same sentence, 'God' also functions as a description. Thus, especially in philosophical language, but also in catechism explanations or theology, one says "By 'God' I mean the infinite Creator of all things," or "I will prove that God exists." The latter proposition means, of course, "I will prove that something exists which verifies the meaning or the description understood by the term 'God.' "

The analysts argue that religious people and theistic philosophers cannot have it both ways. They must use 'God' either as a name or as a description, but not as both. Since, in fact, they do use both they never know exactly what they are doing, especially since they give no warning that they are shifting from one use to another or any hint that they are aware of so doing. Hence, they do not realize that they are talking nonsense as long as they continue to talk only about God. This does not appear until one introduces examples from ordinary language into the forms of language applied to God, at which point the nonsense suddenly emerges into the open. Thus it would be clearly absurd to say in ordinary language, "John means a rational animal," or "I will prove that John exists."[9]

This objection does not seem to be a very difficult one to handle, though many analysts make a great deal of it and one who is not used to their kind of thinking can easily be confused when first encountering this type of objection. It is quite possible to use a term correctly and meaningfully in practice and yet not be able to give the correct explicit analysis of what one is actually doing. The present instance is a perfect case in point. In several different groups to whom I have spoken on this subject I have asked the audience without warning to choose which function, name, or description they thought corresponded best to their own actual usage. In every case roughly one-half voted for name, the other for description, and each was surprised at the other.

Analysts themselves are divided on the issue. Many, including most of those who deny the meaningfulness of language about God, insist that it really functions as a name. My own view and that of I. M. Bochenski, O.P.,[10] the universally esteemed logician, is that if one accepts this position he places himself in a most uncomfortable

---

9 See especially #22, where this objection occupies a large part of the book; also the essay of Paul Ziff, "About 'God,' " in Sidney Hook, ed., *Religious Experience and Truth* (New York: New York Univ. Press, 1961), pp. 195-202.

10 I. Bochenski, "Some Problems for a Philosophy of Religion," *ibid.*, pp. 48-54, and my own brief comment on Ziff's paper, pp. 224-25.

corner in which he will have considerable difficulty in clearing himself of the charge of linguistic and conceptual confusion.

It would seem that the term 'God' functions rather as a description than as a name. The decisive evidence is that one can always ask, "What does 'God' mean?" and give an answer in terms of a description. This would be impossible if the term were really being used as a proper name. True, it is a description of a rather special sort, yet not without some parallels in ordinary language. Because its meaning allows it to be verified by only a single referent, one can gradually come to drop the article, which originally accompanied the term 'god' like any other description. Thus one begins to use it as a convenient substitute for a name in direct address: "O God. . . ." The same occasionally is done with other descriptive terms that have only one referent. Thus one can say in religious or even poetic discourse, "O Sun, warm us with thy rays this day," or "O moon. . . ."

One reason for this double usage is that strictly speaking—at least in the West since the Judaeo-Christian monotheistic tradition, we have had no proper name for God. Nor do we wish to give him one, since he cannot be pointed out or defined and does not need to be distinguished from other presumably real gods, as in polytheistic paganism.

But whatever solution one adopts, one lesson should emerge from this first brief encounter with linguistic analysis: that of the rich complexity and uniqueness of language—and therefore of thought—about God. This manifests the care with which one must explain what he is actually doing when speaking about him and how easy it is to get mixed up in such attempts at explanation.

God as 'Necessary Being.' A second and more difficult challenge is that which maintains that the traditional description of God as 'necessary Being' is meaningless: a flagrant example of a "category mistake" or linguistic muddle. The term 'necessary' in modern logic and semantics has been clearly identified as a modal term referring to propositions, not directly to things. It is used properly when one says, for example, "It is necessary that X is Y," or " 'X is Y' is a necessary proposition," or " 'X is Y' cannot not be true," and possibly even " 'God exists' is a necessary proposition." But it is nonsense to say "God is a necessary Being," just as it would be to say, "God is a declarative being, an analytic being, or a proposition."[11]

---

[11] Several essays in #19 take up this point, pro and con. John Hick defends the use of the term to indicate necessity of fact only, #31. Cf. also #18.

There are several ways of trying to answer this. One is to admit that 'God is a necessary Being' is really only a shorthand expression for " 'God exists' is a necessary proposition." However, this leads one into serious trouble, for strictly speaking a 'necessary proposition' means an analytic proposition whose truth is self-evident from the mere analysis of the terms. Surely one could not hold that in this case, unless he held either the ontological argument or some immediate intuition of the divine essence here below.

Others have held that 'God exists' is a necessary proposition in the sense of being necessarily true as a conclusion from the fact that creatures exist. But this terminology is not successful, for all it means is that the proposition 'God exists' follows necessarily from the proposition 'creatures exist.' However, just because one proposition follows necessarily from another does not make the former a necessary proposition in the strict and proper sense of the term. The analysts are correct in affirming that no existential proposition can be a necessary or analytic proposition for man, except perhaps and for very special reasons the proposition 'I exist.'

Others have followed what seems a wiser course. They maintain that just because modern logicians have agreed on the meaning of 'necessary' as a term referring to propositions only does not imply that this is the only possible meaning of the term throughout the history of philosophy. The traditional meaning of 'necessary being' has been this: a being which cannot not exist. There is no intrinsic reason why such a meaning, if consistently adhered to and clearly specified, is not a legitimate one. It would have as much claim to acceptance as the modern logical one, though the latter may be more convenient at present for a variety of other reasons, partly due to changing conventions.

One must be careful, however, in interpreting the above definition. 'Cannot not exist' can never be taken in an absolute and unconditioned sense, as though self-contained and independent of all other propositions or truths. For man in this life it can only mean: God cannot not exist, granted that one knows that creatures exist and imply God as their necessary condition of possibility. Remove one's knowledge of creatures as the point of departure or of reference, and one's knowledge of God's existence, except for special direct mystical knowledge, also disappears. Hence the necessity of God's existence as known by us is never known as a necessary proposition by itself, but only as a necessary conclusion of another contingent proposition, "Creatures, or finite things, exist." If creatures, then God; but creatures; therefore God.

Such necessity is a necessity of fact only, not of essence or *de jure*, because we can never know as an unconditionally necessary proposition that something must exist.[12] We must discover first the fact of some existence and then draw out its necessary implications. This factual necessity, or necessity implied in a non-necessary fact, is quite different from the modern and more strict understanding of 'necessary.' Hence it is not clear that much is gained any longer in using this terminology of 'necessary being' as applied to God.

It is noteworthy that St. Thomas himself never uses it as an attribute proper to God.[13] This came in only through the Augustinian tradition stemming from Anselm. It became fixed as a primary attribute of God only in modern scholasticism through which it spread to other modern philosophers in the rationalist tradition which tended to deduce or at least explain the existence of God as somehow flowing from his essence. Duns Scotus is a prime example of this procedure, even though he stays clear of the ontological argument in its pure form. St. Thomas in no way deduces the existence of God from his essence, but rather defines his essence completely in terms of his existence: God is *ipsum Esse Subsistens*, pure subsistent Act of Existence. In a sense he has no essence at all because he has no limiting principle.[14]

It might be argued against the above that once one knows that creatures exist and that therefore God must exist in fact, one can argue that he could never have begun and can never cease to exist. Hence, one knows that by his nature God must always

---

12 See #31.

13 For St. Thomas, 'contingent' and 'necessary' have quite different meanings from their now traditional use in modern philosophy, including modern scholasticism. For him, 'contingent' meant simply any composite of matter and form, any generable and corruptible, whose prime matter could be or not be according to the substantial form it now has. 'Necessary' means just the opposite: any pure form that is not subject to substantial change. Both angels and God are such, God having his necessary being *a se*, not *ab alio*. See T. B. Wright, "Necessary and Contingent Being in St. Thomas," *New Scholasticism*, XXV (1951), 439-66; also T. C. Pater, "The Question of the Validity of the Tertia Via," in J. Ryan, ed., *Studies in Philosophy and the History of Philosophy* (Washington: Catholic Univ. of America Press, 1963), II, 137-77; T. K. Connolly, "The Basis for the Third Proof of the Existence of God," *Thomist*, XVII (1954), 282-379.

14 See my own article on "Aseity," the history of the term *ens a se*, in the forthcoming *New Catholic Encyclopedia*.

exist and cannot not exist. This is quite true in a sense. But what it really affirms is not that there must absolutely be a God in view of what his own nature is, but rather that granted God must exist, his nature must be such that he cannot at any time come into or lose the existence it is already known to have. In a word, granted that he exists, his existence is of the self-sufficient type, independent of any other and hence eternal. 'Self-sufficient' and 'eternal' express this more accurately and with less chance of ambiguity for modern philosophers than 'necessary being.' Nevertheless, if the term is carefully limited to necessity of fact as explained above, it is still quite legitimate in itself and maintains a link with a tradition of modern philosophy and scholasticism, though not with St. Thomas.

One might insist, however, that once one knows that God's essence is to exist, it can be said that his existence is necessary because of his nature. To my mind, this is not at all true. To say "God's essence is to exist, or is his existence" is in no way for human minds the same as, or reducible to, the affirmation "God exists." The first does not mean "God's essence is such that he must exist," for this is something which a man cannot know absolutely in itself. At least for a Thomist it means rather: "Granted that God's essence exists, or supposing that it did, it would have to be pure subsistent act of existing." It is impossible for man's mind to fuse into a single proposition both the existence of an essence and what kind of essence it is. The "logical grammar" of attributive and existential propositions is irreducibly different. Whether or not in the case of God one can fuse the two in a single act of purely intellectual insight is another and very difficult question. Certainly one cannot express this in any human concepts or propositions, let alone in one and the same proposition. To attempt to do so is to lay oneself open to well-nigh unanswerable charges by the analysts of linguistic muddles or category confusions.

In conclusion, it would seem more satisfactory and safe to describe God as 'self-sufficient and eternal' than as 'necessary being.' This is due to the many nasty logical traps that can lurk inside the latter. It is also due to the extreme difficulty in getting modern philosophers to understand the traditional meaning of the term or to abandon their own now strongly rooted usage of 'necessary' as applying to propositions only and not to things.

Falsification Theory of Meaning. The next challenge is based on the so-called "falsification theory of meaning" now very much in vogue among analysts.[15] This is a considerably more subtle and sophisticated successor to the now largely discredited verification theory of meaning proposed by the logical positivists, as noted earlier. The latter was a crudely empiricist criterion. Whether or not the former is only an undercover variation of the latter in more refined and moderate terms, as some maintain, is still very much a subject of dispute.

According to the falsification principle of meaning, a term or proposition has no meaning unless it is possible to specify what its opposite would be, in the case of a term or concept, or what would falsify it, in the case of a proposition. In a word, to be meaningful necessarily implies excluding some other meaning or possible state of affairs. For example, suppose one were to say, "X is a loving husband," and then someone objected that X beats his wife regularly, humiliates her in public, does not provide for her, and has affairs with other women. Now, if no matter what facts about the behavior of X were brought up, one kept answering, "Oh, that is compatible with what I mean by a good husband," the original statement would have been without meaning. In other words, if one refuses to accept any state of affairs at all as falsifying or counting against the truth of an assertion, then the statement becomes meaningless or vacuous. If it excludes no possible state of affairs, then it adds no distinguishable intelligible content and becomes indistinguishable from asserting "X is a husband," or even "X is a bad husband."

There is clearly something to this principle, as the example shows. It is particularly useful for judging the fruitfulness of scientific theories and concepts. An hypothesis or theory which no possible experiment could falsify would be completely useless to a scientist, since there would be no way to test it. No definite predictions could be made from it, since all possible outcomes would be equally compatible with it. It is also clear that it applies quite generally to all particular or restrictive concepts which distinguish one thing from another. The crucial question is whether it applies absolutely and necessarily to all concepts and propositions, no matter how universal and ultimate, such as being or God.

This principle might be applied to propositions about God. One says that God is an all-loving, all-provident Father. In the case of a human father one can test an assertion like this by specifying cer-

---

15 See especially Flew's essay in #19 and the answers to it.

tain falsifying conditions which, if verified, would lead one to judge that the statement was false. For example, he might allow his children to be tortured, starved, or injured in accidents when he could prevent these misfortunes. However, when one applies this test to God and asks the believer to specify what he would consider as decisive evidence counting against his belief in God's love or providence towards himself or other men, he discovers that the believer suddenly refuses to play the game or keeps changing the rules. He is quite willing to point to various events in his life, such as escaping death by an improbable chance, as marks of God's providence. But when asked, "Well, suppose you, or your children, had not been so spared; suppose this or this or this disaster had happened to them or you, would this have meant that God did not love or watch over you?," the truly committed believer always answers, "Oh no, that too would come under God's providence, only in a more hidden way."

If one keeps on this way, it turns out that no matter how one heaps up disasters of the most catastrophic and heart-rending nature the believer on principle will not accept any possible specifiable state of this universe as telling decisively against his belief that God is provident and loving. In that case, the analysts conclude, his propositions have become meaningless, because vacuous. Their terms no longer bear any recognizable resemblance to the original meaning they had in the ordinary language situations which gave them birth. In fact, they have no specifiable meaning at all. To say, "The universe is governed by divine providence or love" now becomes indistinguishable from saying, "The universe is the way it is," or "Things happen the way they happen." 'Providence' now means nothing more than whatever way things actually happen. So it is with other divine attributes. Their attribution to God becomes, not false, but simply empty of all meaning.

This presents a most salutary challenge to the depth and accuracy of one's understanding of just what he does or should mean when he makes such statements about God. Two main avenues of response lie open and have been followed up by theistic philosophers. One is to accept the falsification theory of meaning, and then locate the falsifying (or verifying) conditions in the next life. When confronted with this type of response, many analysts suddenly bring into the open the hidden empiricist bias or presuppositions underlying their thought by insisting that the falsifying evidence must lie in some empirically describable state of affairs in this life. Their reasons are that one can know nothing about conditions in another life, if there is one, nor can one even speak meaningfully at all about personal survival in a mode of life unimaginably different from this which one's whole language has been built to express.

But even when this hidden empiricist limitation on what will be accepted as evidence is not insisted upon, it is no easy job to specify now just what the absolutely decisive falsifying (or verifying) conditions in another life would be for divine providence or love. An other-worldly empirical test for the divine attributes is no easy thing to lay down. Somehow one's religious and psychological instincts indicate that it would be possible to know that it is not all a hoax. But there are peculiar logical and conceptual difficulties in formulating this clearly. Analysts would seem to have had somewhat the better of it in their arguments with theists who have attempted this path.[16]

The other and preferable way of responding to the objection is to refuse absolutely to accept any empirical test for or against the attributes of God, above all in this life. The truly religious believer must first make a total loving commitment of himself to God as the kind of being or person one can and should completely trust. Then one believes firmly that God will be infinitely loving and provident over him in all things simply because he believes that God is this kind of being. One has made a total commitment to Him, giving Him a complete blank check, so to speak, as to just *how* He chooses to execute in detail this providence. In other words, one trusts ahead of time that everything will be under God's providence for one's good, without laying down any humanly conceived empirical conditions or tests by which His love will be judged.

Of course some adequate humanly reasonable evidence, either through argument, personal religious experience, or the evaluation of the trustworthiness of some revealing messenger (Christ), is needed in order to hold that God exists as God, that He is of such a nature as to deserve one's total commitment. But once this

<hr />

[16] John Hick has attempted to defend a verification in the next life: #24, and "Theology and Verification," *Theology Today*, XVII (1960), 12-31. See the answer of Kai Nielsen, "Eschatological Verification," *Canadian Journal of Theology*, IX (1963), 271-81, and his acidly critical attack on the meaningfulness of language about God in general, "On Speaking of God," *Theoria*, XXVIII (1962), 110-37.

is believed any such cautious empirical calculations based on our finite human reason would be quite out of place within the authentic religious attitude. They would, in fact, be equivalent to a kind of practical atheism or unbelief.

Similarly the theistic philosopher will refuse on principle to lay down any empirical falsifying or verifying conditions for the divine attributes. He will assert them simply because they follow by a priori metaphysical necessity once the existence of an infinitely perfect Creator of all things has been established. If there is a God at all, then one can and should assert that He must be infinitely loving and providential. To do otherwise would be to contradict His nature. One does not and cannot know from human reason alone just what these attributes mean in any concretely specifiable empirical detail. This would require a knowledge of the infinite wisdom and power of God equal to His own knowledge of Himself, and on the face of it this would be a contradiction. Hence, if one understands properly the nature of man's knowledge of God, he should not attempt to inject any determinate empirical content at all into his concepts about God or His attributes. There is only an indeterminate analogical pointing to an unspecifiable infinitely "Better" than all one knows in experience.

The great fruitfulness of coming to grips with an objection like this is that it exposes any hidden empiricism in one's philosophical thinking or religious attitudes with respect to God. When put to such a test, many apparently quite religious people find that their belief in God's providence or love has actually been based or conditioned more than they realized on a concealed empirical test such as: when they prayed a certain piece of good fortune befell them or a certain disaster was averted from themselves or their dear ones. When it turns out that one of their implicitly accepted falsifying conditions does actually become verified, they then revolt against God or even reject His existence, saying "This I will not accept, this is the limit of my endurance," or "I cannot believe that God would allow this to happen to me; hence He cannot exist."

This attitude resembles much more the Roman legal-contractual type of religion, "Do ut des" (I offer you this sacrifice in order that you give me this favor in return), than authentic Christianity or genuine personal religion of any kind. This searching challenge of the analysts in the name of the falsification principle of meaning can force one to clarify both the quality of his religious belief and

his understanding of just what he does mean when he speaks of
the various attributes of God.

How Give Meaning to Predicates about God? The next and last
main challenge is a very general and fundamental one. It undoubtedly gives the most trouble to contemporary analytic-minded philosophers, including theists, when they try to make sense, or, as they
say, "do the analysis," of language about God. It is the difficulty of
showing how any definite specifiable meaning can be given to
language about God, including not only attributes like 'personal,'
and 'loving,' but also the basic proposition itself, "God exists.'

The objection arises from a consideration of the general way
in which meaning is given to terms. For purely formal logical and
mathematical terms, meaning is stipulated by construction and is
not intended to describe any real entities. But all terms describing
real entities must be derived from some mode of human experience
in dealing with the world and ourselves, in which is included scientific experimentation. Their meaning depends on their usage in
some one of the established "language games" or ways in which men
express their various modes of contact with reality.

The trouble with metaphysical language in general and language about God in particular is that it takes terms endowed with
meanings derived from one language game, predominantly ordinary
experience, and shifts them to express something notably different,
in fact infinitely beyond, their original referents. In so doing it
necessarily modifies their original meaning. The difficulty which
arises is how one might give meaningful content to the new aspect
or dimension of the old meaning. The source cannot be the same
as that of the old meaning, one's own experience, because that is
just what one is transcending in this new application and the very
reason why the meaning is being partly changed. It cannot be the
new dimension of reality, because it is by definition beyond one's
experience. It cannot be constructed, since all construction is based
on materials derived originally from experience, and everything in
God is by definition infinitely beyond and other than one's experience. Neither can it be experimentally tested in any way. Hence
the new meaning given to terms in order to apply them to
something beyond one's experience, like God, turns out to be
irremediably vacuous.

The device of analogy cannot be of any real help in this case.
An analogous term is one that, according to the standard definition,

is applied to several subjects according to a meaning partly the same and partly different in each case. This is all very well when one can know directly in themselves all of the subjects to which one applies the term. By direct comparison of the referents among themselves one can control the partial changes in meaning in the different cases. But in the case of God one cannot at all know him directly or properly as he is in himself. Hence one cannot compare him with the other analogates in order to determine just how the meaning of the analogous term differs when applied to Him.

The famous Thomistic analogy of proper proportionality is of no assistance whatsoever here. All it tells one is that God's existence, knowledge, or love is proportioned to His essence, just as anyone's characteristics are proportioned to his essence. This is true but trivial since it delivers only a purely formal relation, empty of any specifiable content, and with no rule for determining what the terms used could possibly mean as realized in God.

The conclusion of all this is, the analysts claim, that neither theistic philosophers nor religious people know what they really mean when they talk about God. Some analysts conclude from this that language about God is simply meaningless. Others note that it must have some meaning because religious, though not philosophical, language has for a long time been a lived language game.

This positive meaning is then variously interpreted. The most common interpretation is that religious language, though ostensibly about God as some entity other than the worshipper, is really only an indirect description of the worshipper's own feelings and attitudes, or characteristic external expressions of these inner dispositions. Thus when the worshipper says, "God is the Supreme Being, my loving Father, and good," what his language really means, whether he understands it or not, is "I have feelings, and perform corresponding ritual actions, of adoration, submission, trust, and prayer," or, in general, "I behave thus, and do these actions with these inner feelings."[17]

This fundamental difficulty is further compounded by the demand made by most analysts as a general principle of meaning analysis. They demand that the meaning of such terms as 'God,' 'exists,' 'infinite,' and 'infinitely good' as applied to God be clearly analyzed and defined before any process of proving that God exists or possesses such and such attributes is undertaken. First tell

[17] See #25.

me, says the analyst, just what 'God' means and how this content carries genuine meaning, before starting to prove that such a being exists. Otherwise one never knows just what he is trying to prove or whether one has succeeded.

The Meaning of Religious Knowledge

This is the general and rather formidable indictment. In sketching out the possibilities of answering it, it will be well to proceed from the easier to the more difficult items.

The Subject. The attempt to analyze the meaning of religious language as being really about the worshipper, not about the worshipped or God himself, is clearly unsuccessful. Many analysts themselves have seen this and many other philosophers, particularly phenomenologists, have underlined it. The reason is simple and decisive. The meaning of religious language in this theory simply is not that intended by the people who actually use the language. Whether mistakenly or not, the religious believer who speaks about God and addresses Him in prayer is firmly convinced that he is speaking about and to a real entity quite independent of and superior to himself. This is what he intends to do by his language; it is the meaning given to it by the user. It would be a model of defective philosophical analysis of language, which is intended to bring out the meaning of the language as lived, if it were to go explicitly counter to the meaning intended by the use in favor of one held only by interpreters who are themselves not participants in the language game. One simple test is the fact that no religious person who accepted this analysis as correct could any longer with psychological integrity and sincerity go on using the language as he did before.

The Terms. The demand by analysts that the meanings of the term 'God' and of the various attributes as applied to Him must be defined clearly first, before proceeding to prove His existence or His possession of these attributes, must be rejected on principle by theistic philosophers. This procedure of precise definition of terms is quite appropriate to logic, mathematics, most areas of science, and many other domains of human thought and discourse, including not a few areas of philosophy.

It is an a priori and totalitarian type of analysis to insist that all proofs in whatever field must always proceed rigidly by this same identical method. This does not do justice to the special, open, heuristic type of concepts that must be, and habitually are used in pushing the frontiers of experience into new and hitherto unexplored areas or in probing hypothetically into areas of causes hidden beyond one's experience. The exploration beyond our present frontiers is essential to the continued expansion of human horizons characteristic of man throughout his history, and especially of modern man. This cannot be done without the systematic use of intentionally open, partly indeterminate, heuristic concepts, or, as it has been put, without "the systematic use of vague language."

In the case of God, the precise meaning of the term appears only at the end of the proof and in function of it. This meaning is elaborated through the very working out of the proof and the term 'God' is really only a concise summary of the conclusion of the proof itself. The proper philosophical approach to discovering or proving the existence of God is not to ask, "Can I prove the existence of God?" This would be to come by the word of another upon an already existing dispute, rather than to come to grips directly with the problem as it presents itself in authentic philosophical fashion.

The proper mode of procedure is to start with the world of one's experience and ask concerning the necessary conditions of possibility for explaining its existence and nature. The first step is to show that this whole finite world cannot contain within itself the sufficient reason for its own existence. As outlined in a previous section above, the principle of sufficient reason or intelligibility is the dynamo of one's whole intellectual life and to it one should have made a fundamental commitment. If one is not to jettison this he must make the basic inference that there must be some adequate explanatory cause somewhere in reality "above" and distinct from (that is, transcending) this world-to-be-explained.

One now proceeds by heuristic concepts, somewhat as is done in mathematics when undertaking to solve a problem. "Let X be the real entity which is needed to solve this problem, possessing whatever properties or attributes are required to fulfill this function." Then the properties of this not directly known or experienceable X are gradually filled in by postulates, one by one, as the indispensable requirements for a solution of the problem appear. Each property of X is determined exclusively by the necessary relation of X to the datum-to-be-explained, that is, by its function in the solution of the problem. If X did not possess something equivalent to such and such a property, with these minimum requirements, then it could be shown clearly that the problem would be insoluble in principle or the solution internally contradictory. Hence, one postulates all these minimum requirements in one's already postulated X, knowing only that they must be present in it in some way, but not knowing or having to know in any determinate or determinable way just how they are present.

One can, of course, start off with a vague nominal definition of what one hopes to reach, drawn not from the problem itself but from some outside pre-existing religious or philosophical belief held by men. But it is clearly impossible and unreasonable to ask for a clear detailing of the properties of the X that solves a problem before actually working out the solution to the problem![18]

The Development of Positive Meaning. With these preliminary roadblocks out of the way, one is left with the central, but now more manageable problem of how one actually does attribute positive meaning to one's language about God in terms of the above process. Here the analysts have the right to demand a much more precise, complete, and especially more concrete and experiential analysis of just what procedure religious people and theistic philosophers actually follow when they speak of God as good, or loving, or Father, or ultimate cause, or Creator.

One is accustomed to propound technical theories of analogy in all kinds of learned discussions. But as for myself, I will honestly admit that it was only recently that I awoke, to my embarrassment and under the challenge of linguistic analysis, to the following situation. For years I had been teaching a doctrine of Thomistic analogy, and many of my students could repeat it and explain it quite accurately. Nevertheless, I had never really asked either myself or them pointblank, "Come now, forget all your abstract theories of predication and analogy, what do you yourself actually do, what do you in the concrete actually mean, and what concrete psychological process do you go through, when you call God 'good,' or 'loving,' or 'infinitely wise,' or 'ultimate cause'?" Without this phenomenological analysis of the actual meaning-giving process at work in religious and philosophical language about God not much progress will be made in contacting and satisfying most modern thinkers. On the other hand a surprising amount of light would

---

[18] The notion and role of heuristic concepts are given central importance by B. Lonergan throughout his *Insight* (New York: Philosophical Library, 1956), and elsewhere in his writings.

emerge for all concerned, including traditional theists, from such an analysis.

In the space remaining this process obviously could not be worked out in detail. In fact, a great deal more comparative work in religious psychology will undoubtedly have to be done before the full phenomenological process can be adequately analyzed. What follows is a general sketch of the main lines of the philosophical process. The above contains enough suggestions as to how the basic notion of ultimate cause would be given meaning. 'Cause' would be given the deliberately vague and general heuristic meaning of whatever it is that is ultimately (that is, with no further relevant questions remaining to be asked) and adequately *responsible* for the actual existence and nature of the datum-to-be-explained: the finite, changing, material universe of our experience. Presuming the basic causal relation established, without which no attributes could be predicated of God from our experience, it is now possible to develop in a little more detail how some of the standard attributes can be given meaning.

First, one discovers some property of things of one's experience which are judged to be a "perfection," that is, better had than not had at all. This is then subjected to the traditional process of "purification," that is, examined as to whether in its very meaning it necessarily implies some limitation, imperfection, or negation of further positive perfection. When one has gone through this process of sifting and testing for intrinsic imperfection the various positive properties of the things known, one concludes with basic values (or attributes of which one can approve):

(a) which are purely positive (containing no negations);

(b) to which one finds that he can and must give unqualified or unconditioned approval, so that one finds himself rationally constrained to judge that it is absolutely better to have them in the highest degree;

(c) which one finds susceptible of degrees of intensity or perfection which cannot be closed off or limited at the top short of an unrestricted plenitude (whatever this might be); and, finally,

(d) which one very much desires to possess oneself in the highest degree possible.

All these "pure" perfections turn out to be reducible to the following: existence, knowledge, love or loving will, and power. These, in fact, are the basic values or standards in terms of which one evaluates everything else. One calls 'good' anyone or all together of these considered in relation to the will as approving. To deny any one of these as an unconditionally affirmed value would be to go against one's human nature, rendering impossible one of the characteristically human modes of evaluation and hence of reasonable action.

Application to God. The next crucial step is to apply to God those basic value-attributes which have been sifted out and purified. Here, it is essential to introduce the dynamism of the intellect and will towards the infinite in order to ground the meaning-giving process. This is also rarely done in elucidating analogous predications of God. Reflecting on the above-mentioned basic value-attributes, one notices two things about one's relation to them. First, one tends strongly toward them or, if you wish, towards one's fulfillment through them. There is such a deep natural desire of one's whole intellectual-willing being, that one cannot not desire them without renouncing one's own deeper self. Secondly, one discovers that their degree of presence both in oneself and in all the finite things one has experienced or can conceive is radically incomplete, defective, and disproportionate to one's deepest inner longing. In a word, a person experiences their limited realization in the things around him, their falling short of the ideal realization which alone would satisfy his yearning.

Every experience or realization of a limit immediately implies a movement of transcendence beyond the limit, a transcending intention towards a beyond by that which is aware of the limit. The existence of an ultimate X which is the ultimate responsible 'cause' of this world and of oneself, and thus the final goal of all one's dynamisms, has already been postulated. Hence, one now makes the crucial act of projection of one's basic values beyond the present limited and unsatisfying degrees in which one finds them and onto the Ultimate, removing all limits and deficiencies as one does so. In this act of projection one does not at all attain any act of perception, intellectual grasp, representation, or comprehension of what this state or perfect realization in the ultimate X at the other end is like in itself, distinctly, and positively. One points to it off in the darkness, so to speak.

This very transcending dynamism which enables one to point

meaningfully beyond one's experience and all finitude, as not coming up to the demands of one's innate and ineradicable desire for fulfillment, enables one to sketch out dimly, in silhouette, or reverse image so to speak (through negations but not aiming at negations), the hidden positive state of plenitude in what one calls 'God.' Above all, and here is the crucial point, it permits one to affirm positively that these values must be realized beyond limitation in God, even though one can get no conception of how.

This is not a mere blind leap into the dark, though it is indeed a leap into the conceptual darkness of the "cloud of unknowing." The positive element which grounds one's projection of meaning onto an entity beyond one's experience, is drawn from one's own experience. It is precisely the unique experience of dynamically transcending the limited, deficient realization of basic values around and in one, understood explicitly or implicitly as limited, deficient, and falling short of one's deep and ineluctable expectations. The very awareness of the gap between the unlimited scope of the intellectual and voluntary desire and the deficient realizations it encounters enables one in some mysterious and indirect way, which can only be experienced rather than abstractly argued about, to know what it is one is looking for, what must be hidden in that ultimate Beyond.

In a word, this is a process of knowing what one is looking for by knowing what one is not yet satisfied with; of knowing what one does want by knowing what one does not want; and of knowing what one means and affirming it by knowing what does not yet exhaust the richness of the meaning that one intends dynamically and obscurely, but positively. As Pascal put it, "Lord, I could not have sought you unless I had already in some way found you." One has no right to neglect such a profound and authentically human experience in one's analysis of the process of human meaning-giving.

The concepts used in this process must all be open-ended ones, with floors or lower limits but no ceilings or upper limits and hence adjusting flexibly to fit the level of whatever the subject of which they are predicated. The predications made by means of them do not pretend to represent how God possesses the perfections signified at His own level. They merely point through these predicates, as though down a series of corridors without limits at the farther end. The predications affirm that God is somewhere along the line or in the direction indicated by these unqualified perfections or values. They serve not as portraits but as windows or doors opening out from within the limited walls of this human habitation onto unlimited perspectives where one's vision finally fails in a blur of light and mist.

Though one does not know just what lies out there waiting for one, he does know unerringly by his judgment of imperfection on all the degrees of realization of these values around him that along this line lies one's fulfillment. It is an unqualifiedly better-than-here, the unqualifiedly best, that in whose presence and communion I want to be with the deepest longing of my nature. This is indeed a positive knowledge of God, but of a very special, mysterious, and trans-conceptual kind. It is a knowledge not through representation but through what is implicit in an innate dynamic tendency which cannot be contained within any given or conceivable limits recognized as limits. The above notion of predications or affirmations which point through open-ended concepts is to my mind the indispensable key to one's legitimate development of meaning for human language about God.[19]

Analogy. It will surely not have escaped the reader's notice that the doctrine of analogy was nowhere mentioned in the preceding analysis. Yet those who know the technical doctrine will certainly realize that its basic content was present implicitly or equivalently throughout. The reason for not appealing explicitly to the traditional Thomistic theory as the answer to the analysts' difficulties is the painful but undeniable fact that this so-called traditional Thomistic doctrine has singularly failed to impress analysts, both theists and otherwise, as shedding any really helpful light on their problems. There are several reasons for this. One is that the theory is enveloped in such unfamiliar technical terms that access to it by most is rendered very difficult. Another is that for many it seems to be inextricably tied up with further characteristically Thomistic

---

[19] A similar use of pointing concepts to refer to the self or subjectivity as such of myself and other persons is made by R. Johann, "Subjectivity," *Review of Metaphysics,* XII (1958), 200-234. It should be obvious that in the analysis I have made above I am strongly indebted to the notion of dynamism of intellect and will toward the infinite as developed by E. Coreth, *Metaphysik* (Innsbruck: Tyrolia, 1961); J. Lotz, *Metaphysica operationis humanae* (Romae: Univ. Gregorianae, 1958); J. Maréchal, *Point de départ de la métaphysique,* V (Paris: Desclée de Brouwer, 1949); and K. Rahner, *Geist in Welt* (München: Kosel-Verlag, 1957). How one can obscurely know the good by one's very tendency toward it is brought out well in the profound article of J. de Finance, "La motion du bien," *Gregorianum,* XXXIX (1958), 5-42.

metaphysical doctrines, such as the real distinction between essence and existence, participation, and causality, which they find it impossible to either understand or be committed to.

However, there is also another and stronger reason which must be faced. That is the serious deficiency in the till recently most widely accepted "traditional" interpretation of Thomistic analogy according to the proper proportionality theory of Cajetan. As mentioned briefly in an earlier section of this paper, if taken by itself, this theory leaves one in almost total agnosticism as to the positive content of the analogous term as applied to God. It offers no rule justifying the actual application of an analogous term to God or giving some positive content to its meaning in this case. Granted that the above two steps have already been established, it then gives a formal rule governing the proportional variability of the meaning-content according to the various subjects of which it is predicated. Given that God is good and that this has some legitimate meaning as applied to God then, since one has explicated this meaning as a relational or proportional one, he knows that the degree and mode of the divine goodness or other attributes will be proportional to His essence. But it is the first two steps that the analysts consider crucial. Hence they consider the proper proportionality doctrine as perhaps true, but trivial as regards the solution of what they deem the really important problems of elucidating the meaningfulness of language about God. There is a good deal of truth in their contention.

This last remark may seem hardly loyal to the Thomistic tradition. But it should by now be no secret to a professional Catholic philosopher that a striking coincidence—since there seems to have been no direct influence—took place at the time that the analysts for their own reasons were finding wanting what they took to be the traditional Thomistic doctrine. At that same time contemporary Thomistic scholars, in one of the most rapid and profound shifts of interpretation in the history of modern Thomism, were coming to the conclusion, on both historical and systematic grounds, that the so-called "traditional" doctrine of Cajetan was both seriously defective in itself and not actually the mature position of St. Thomas himself.

Leading scholars, such as Lyttkens, Klubertanz, and most recently and decisively Montagnes, have now drawn massive support behind the thesis that St. Thomas, after making use of the structure of proper proportionality in only two or three places in his earliest works, quietly abandoned it thereafter as too agnostic to adequately justify one's predications about God. He substituted for it the much richer and more soundly metaphysically grounded doctrine of the analogy of participation, or of causal participation as it is now commonly called. This is built on the explicit reference to a single causal source that possesses a given perfection in plenitude and communicates it by causation to many different recipients according to varying degrees of intensive participation.[20]

Most analysts do not seem aware of this recent highly significant development in Thomistic thought. Further, the subject is still so clouded in intra-school technical disputes and metaphysical terminology that one could hardly expect outsiders at present to find their way easily through this technical tangle. Even if they did, however, in addition to this general doctrine of analogous predication based on causal participation, they would legitimately demand a much more concrete and detailed psychological, phenomenological, and logical-semantic analysis of just what goes on in the process of giving meaning to terms predicated analogously of God. They would want to know just how the users of this language actually understand and concretely carry out the process from within.

The full analysis of the above process in its concrete totality would use all the resources, not only of metaphysics, but of modern semantics, phenomenological analysis, and symbolism theory. This seems to me one of the most worthwhile and urgent tasks now facing Thomistic and all theistic philosophers if they wish to make vital contact with contemporary needs and solve the problems in their own right. This constitutes a strong invitation to participate in this task of collaboration.

---

[20] See the key works: G. Klubertanz, *St. Thomas Aquinas on Analogy* (Chicago: Loyola Univ. Press, 1960), with its copious bibliography, and the recent widely praised B. Montagnes, *L'analogie de l'être d'après S. Thomas d'Aquin* (Louvain: Nauwelaerts, 1964).

SELECTED BIBLIOGRAPHY

1. Charlesworth, Maxwell. *Philosophy and Linguistic Analysis*. Pittsburgh: Duquesne Univ. Press, 1959.

2. ————. *Logical Positivism*. Glencoe: Free Press, 1959. Valuable collection of articles by various authors; long bibliography including much linguistic analysis.

3. Ayer, A. J., *et al*. *The Revolution in Philosophy*. London: Macmillan, 1956. High level popular lectures on BBC; key phases of new movement.

4. Flew, A., ed. *Logic and Language*. New York: Philosophical Library, 1951. Representative essays by "ordinary language school." 2nd Series, 1955.

5. "Symposium: What is Philosophy?" *Proceedings of the Aristotelian Society, Supplement*, XI (1932), 23-67.

6. "Symposium: Is Analysis a Useful Method in Philosophy?" *ibid.*, XIII (1934), 53-118.

7. "Symposium: The Nature of Analysis," *Journal of Philosophy*, LIV (1957), 741-66.

8. Ryle, G. *The Concept of Mind*. New York: Barnes and Noble, 1949. Classic example of analysis.

9. ————. *Dilemmas*. Cambridge: Cambridge Univ. Press, 1954.

10. Waismann, F. "How I see Philosophy," in *Contemporary British Philosophy*. 3rd Series. Edited by H. D. Lewis. London: Allen and Unwin, 1956, pp. 445-90. Key exposé of analysis.

11. Rorty, R. "Realism, Categories, and the 'Linguistic Turn'," *International Philosophical Quarterly*, II (1962), 307-22. Warning to realist metaphysicians not to attack linguistic analysts because they reach the same conclusions in different language.

12. Caton, C. E., ed. *Philosophy and Ordinary Language*. Urbana: Univ. of Illinois Press, 1963. Valuable collection of famous articles.

13. Lewis, H. D., ed. *Clarity Is Not Enough: Essays in Criticism of Linguistic Philosophy*. New York: Humanities Press, 1963.

14. Weitz, Morris. "Oxford Philosophy," *Philosophical Review*, LXXII (1953), 187-234. Fine introduction to what the school is doing and why it is significant, with examples.

15. Ferré, Fred. *Language, Logic and God*. New York: Harper, 1961. Survey of whole controversy, with good bibliography. Defends language about God.

16. Charlesworth, M. "Linguistic Analysis and Language about God," *International Philosophical Quarterly*, I (1961), 139-67. Good survey with bibliographical references.

17. Collins, J. "Analytic Theism and Demonstrative Inference," *ibid.*, 235-63. Discussion of rejection of proofs typical of analysts.

18. Clarke, W. N., S.J. "Linguistic Analysis and Natural Theology," *Proceedings of the American Catholic Philosophical Association*, XXXIV (1960), 110-26. Survey of question and sketch of responses.

19. Flew, A. and MacIntyre, A. *New Essays in Philosophical Theology*. London: SCM Press, 1955. Opening of the present controversy.

20. Hepburn, Ronald. *Christianity and Paradox*. London: Watts, 1958. Sharp challenge to the intelligibility of Christian language; one of the most astute.

21. Ramsey, Ian. *Religious Language*. London: SCM, 1957. Attempt of an Anglican philosopher-theologian to meet attack. Abandons all metaphysical language, to save faith. Aroused considerable dissatisfaction among theists.

22. Martin, C. *Religious Belief*. Ithaca, N.Y.: Cornell Univ. Press, 1961. Sharp attack on meaningfulness of theistic language.

23. Mitchell, Basil, ed. *Faith and Logic*. London: Allen and Unwin, 1957. Essays by Anglican philosophers who agree on faith and the non-relevance of metaphysics, especially of the proofs of natural theology for understanding religion.

24. Hick, John. *Faith and Knowledge*. Ithaca, N.Y.: Cornell Univ. Press, 1957. Defense of meaningfulness of the language of faith and the place of philosophical knowledge about God.

25. Braithwaite, R. *An Empiricist's View of the Nature of Religious Belief*. Cambridge: Cambridge Univ. Press, 1955. Classic attack. Religious language describes attitudes and emotions of believer and ritual, but says nothing about God.

26. Williams, C. J. "Existence and the Meaning of the Word 'God,' " *Downside Review*, LXXVII (1958-1959), 53-71.

27. Blackstone, W. T. *The Problem of Religious Knowledge*. Englewood Cliffs: Prentice-Hall, 1963. Survey of positions.

28. Christian, W. *Meaning and Truth in Religion*. Princeton, N.J.: Princeton Univ. Press, 1964. Positive defense of religious language.

29. Daly, C. B. "The Knowableness of God," *Philosophical Studies* (Maynooth), IX (1959), 90-137. Survey of the whole problem in the contemporary setting.

30. Hick, J., ed. *Faith and the Philosophers*. New York: St. Martin's Press, 1964. Symposium between believers and unbelievers.

31. ————. "God and Necessary Being," *Journal of Philosophy*, LVIII (1961), 725-34. Expanded version, "Necessary Being," *Scottish Journal of Theology*, XIV (1961), 353-69. Defends 'necessity of fact' meaning of traditional expression.

THE INFLUENCE OF A PHENOMENOLOGY OF 'DESCENT' UPON CERTAIN ASPECTS OF THE SPIRITUAL AND THEOLOGICAL

by

WILFRID DESAN

The philosopher who is conversant with, and working in the idiom of these times cannot be indifferent to what phenomenology has thus far produced and to what it is still capable of producing. If he has inherited a new tool, it is his duty to explore all the possible uses of that tool. The purpose of this paper is to explore the nature of the phenomenological method and its possible application to matters theological and spiritual.

Phenomenological Method of 'Ascent'

One might begin with a definition of the phenomenological method in order to make certain that all stand upon common ground. This is especially important since the investigation later will move onto a terrain which has not hitherto been considered part of the phenomenological landscape, and hence has not been amply explored. The phenomenological as here understood is not quite the same as that propagated by the Husserlian tradition. Before leaving the Husserlian common ground, however, this will first be sketched in its contours in a brief two-part examination of what Husserl and Merleau-Ponty and their followers have intended, and to an extent have indeed succeeded in doing. Only then may one ask whether, setting forth on a newer path leading in another direction, one might not do even more.

1. Phenomenology is descriptive and neither Husserl nor any of his followers intended to do anything more. Their avowed aim has not been to interpret that which they confront, but merely to grasp it in its phenomenal appearance. It should be well understood that this intensive analysis of "that which appears" cannot and does not lead to any metaphysical substratum. Indeed, phe-

74

nomenology might even be said to have originated as a reaction against any metaphysical reading of the physical world.

Metaphysics interprets, or at least attempts to interpret, a visible reality. It presupposes that human inquiry can reach some answer, that is, that it can offer a unifying interpretation of the world and of man. Metaphysics is thus the ultimate understanding, since it can be said in the strict sense to reach for the absolute. This search for the absolute has at times had its abuses. Frequently, it was based upon insufficient observation; and, at its worst, it was made with apologetic purposes that took precedence over the observations that were made. Metaphysicians setting forth in this spirit did not want so much to know as to defend and to protect. They wanted to know merely in order to protect that which a certain faith had proposed as revealed truth. Their whole effort, then, consisted in choosing premises that led to preconceived conclusions and in eliminating everything else.

Husserl can be said to be a reaction against that sort of narrowed vision. One observes not only that which one wants to observe, but that which one actually confronts: the redness of a certain color, the hardness of wood, the extension of the body in space, the awareness of space—nothing is excluded. This careful observation of that which appears, although failing to give the great answers of traditional metaphysics, has nevertheless opened the way to some arresting insights.

If the conclusions resulting from phenomenological observation have not advanced the knowledge of such metaphysical concepts as substance, soul, and Deity, they have, on the other hand, provided contemporary man with new images of himself and of his world. One might mention in passing only the outstanding achievements of Sartre and of Merleau-Ponty in that domain: their observations of human consciousness confronting the world of matter that surrounds it; the description of man's attempt to dominate and to organize space; the examination of temporality and the existence of man within a succession of past, present, and future; and the discovery of the amazing position of the human body as a center of reference.

2. It soon became clear that phenomenological research was to require extremely astute observation, for to take notice of "that which appears" does not always imply to accept the immediately obvious. It required an attention in depth which places conscious-

ness at the threshold of a naked world and observes how human intervention confronts this unadulterated matter, drawing it into the orbit of man and giving it meaning. Sartre's *Nausea* is a macabre example of what matter is without man and of how it obtains its beauty or its ugliness through man. The observation of phenomena is inutterably complex, since man himself, be he called *Pour-soi* or *Dasein*, becomes through his encounter with a world, and in the selfsame act the world also becomes. The absolute value of the phenomenologist lies in this becoming in both the act of observation and the state of being observed: the absolute encloses both man and the world in a single embrace. Locked together and inseparable in that encounter are the individual subject or consciousness—the individual making this world—and the world that he makes and that, in being made, makes him.

3. What Husserl had not foreseen is that the precise observation of the surrounding world would not result in the mathematically uniform conclusions for which he had hoped, but instead would explode into a variety. Where the individual subject is the *magister* there are as many worlds as there are *magistri*. Husserl unwittingly reached the pluralistic, and by this very token proved the fragmentary.

It is this fragmentation of the human noesis that deserves attention. In the segmentation of the noesis, it is possible that an ontology may be uncovered that would lead to a closer grasp of the real essence of man, and thus to a metaphysics that escaped when the exploration began from the individual. Husserlian phenomenology attaches itself to the assertion that the individual is an absolute and thus also an absolute starting point. Yet this absolute dimension loses its deeper value if it is not set within an absolute of the ultimate. Only against the background of metaphilosophy, that is, of a total noesis as held by the human totality itself, can the philosophical approach of one individual come into full relief. Only in the recognition of its segmentary noesis can the absolute value of the Husserlian phenomenology gain philosophical status.

The approach of Sartre or Heidegger obtains its real value only through the acceptance of the plural, or the plural as unified in the *totum*. But it is precisely this *totum*, this acceptance of a totality above and beyond the singular, which they, following Husserl, have missed. Hence, they make absolute the "relative" or "personal absolute," with no recognition of that which transcends the individual vision. This recognition is necessary, for however authentic an individual vision may be, it nonetheless shapes each one, not as the whole, but as part of the whole.

At this point the objection might be made that if the individual "absolute" is transcended, and an absolute that is embodied in the *totum* is accepted, the result seems to be a multiplication of absolutes. This is indeed so, but the theory which I wish to propose makes room for this multiplicity, which is seen to exist underneath the span, or cupola, of a transcendent absolute that is embodied in or visualized by the *totum*. Thus, although the individual necessarily thinks of his particular possession as being an absolute, that is, although he absolutizes his love and unwillingly his knowledge of the world as well, these individual absolutes come from the Totality itself. They are a product of the *Totum* and have as their aim the protection of that *totum,* even while receiving their singularity from the individual himself or from what I have elsewhere called the "fragment." The individual, then, in absolutizing his love and his noesis, enhances the whole. But the very recognition of the relative character of the individual performance within this individual "absolute" gives the individual his ontological mark: it stamps him as a fragment.

4. The implications of these remarks are far-reaching. The recognition of the individual as ontological fragment, a moment in time and an atomos in space, is more than an act of self-pity; it is a philosophical attitude. It may very well appear that if the individual is by himself capable only of the "subjective" and of "individual attainment," the acknowledgment of the limited ontological dimension that is his, with the subsequent death of any individual claim to completeness, could open a new vista upon the possibilities of the collective. If the recognition of the fragmentary dimension of the individual is at the birth of the collective, as I believe it is, it naturally follows that it will no longer do to depart from the individual as the *inconcussum.* One must instead depart from the totality conceived as the additive collection of human beings.

Phenomenological Method of 'Descent'

This is a radically new brand of phenomenology. It no longer starts from the *cogito* to constitute what might be called a phenomenology of 'ascent,' but from the totality to constitute what might be called a phenomenology of 'descent.' This phenomenology of 'descent' is still descriptive; but instead of ascending from the individual man as the predominant entity to the totality of men, it comes down from the *totum* to its inner constituents. It is in this descent that the acceptance of the outside periphery is *ipso facto* stated and accepted, and that the totality is acknowledged: whether that *totum* exists now, or was, or will be.

It is, of course, to be understood that my use of the Latin term *totum* or whole points, not to the *totum logicum* or logical class, but rather to the *totum physicum* or physical addition of the plurality of men. Individual man is fragment or part of that *totum*. He comes from it and belongs to it forever; his roots are deep within it, and to it he is irrevocably tied. Man alone and supreme is inconceivable.

All this results in a oneness, a cohesiveness, a tight net of intercourse, intercommunication, interdependence in a multiple form— social, intellectual, biological, economic, and cultural. This is not the place to elaborate on this aspect. It is only necessary to observe that life does build up this oneness of the human totality, and that this oneness results in a global survival of the *totum;* yet this survival of the *totum* is made possible only through its inner fragmentation. The structure of the *totum* is necessarily one of many parts which are spread open in time and space. Although it appears as a Parmenidean *quantum* when looked at from an atemporal point of view, it encompasses within its organic unity a succession of fragments. It is because of this succession that in its internal structure the *totum* can be said to have a past, a future, and a present. The hypothesis of a *totum* existing all at once *(simul et totum)*, that is, without temporal succession or spatial separation, must not be altogether excluded; but this is obviously not the case in this world. The cohesion of the one has not excluded the separation and diversity of the many.

Indeed, the whole technique of the Creator seems to have been the imposition of survival as a categorical imperative upon the *totum* and its realization through the plurality of fragments. This conclusion is important, for in it I believe one reaches the fundamental scheme of human life as known in the natural order. That is, within a space and time universe move human fragments, parts of a gigantic *totum,* which through this fragmentation and the resulting multiplicity and diversity fulfills its purpose: survival.

A Philosophical Example and Its Criticism

Up to now mankind has been considered as a whole; but within that whole there are smaller totalities or groups. Like its ur-model, the group has both diversity and internal oneness. The "oneness" of a group goes hand in hand with its confrontataion of an absolute. This implies that some form of survival, be it temporal or eternal, natural or supernatural, is at stake. Some form of imperative compels the diverse into oneness and thereby molds the group. This absolute may not always be clearly formulated, but it is nevertheless always there. Against a known or unknown background of survival, against some form of disappearance, coalescence starts the one, constitutes it, and causes it to endure.

In his *Critique de la raison dialectique* (1960) Jean-Paul Sartre has made an intensive, extremely penetrating and shrewd examination of group formation. His observations have all been made from the Husserlian point of view, or in other words, with the use of the method which above has been called the phenomenology of 'ascent.'[1] In order to see more clearly the implications of the choice, let us turn to an example taken from Sartre's book.

It is July 12, 1789, and there is a state of insurrection in Paris. Several things may be observed. The Parisians, still juxtaposed simply as members of a series not yet constituting a group, are hungry and tired. Their pleas for a greater equality and a chance to alleviate their misery have gone unheeded by the government. On the contrary, the king and his ministers are set against them, already provoking an embryonic form of unity-in-misery amidst the disunited Parisians. People talk and grumble and begin to move. They discover, furthermore, that the army has encircled Paris. All of these factors—mutual discomfort, the opposition of the government, and the siege of the army—strengthen the cohesion of the people.

The menace now becomes more precise in one section of the city, in the neighborhood of the Bastille, the *quartier* Saint Antoine. Since the inhabitants of this *quartier* must defend themselves both against the enemy in front of them coming from the outside and against the enemy in the rear posted in the Bastille, they are more pressed than the others and must act as a group if they want to

---

[1] Jean-Paul Sartre, *Critique de la raison dialectique* (Paris: Gallimard, 1960). For comment and critical examination, see Wilfrid Desan, *The Marxism of Jean-Paul Sartre* (New York: Doubleday, 1965).

survive. They stream onto the street, and an elementary form of organization begins.

Philosophically (still in the Sartrian view) what happens is this: each one of the inhabitants of the *quartier* Saint Antoine totalizes the event through his very act of participation or praxis of moving onto the street. Each one is himself a synthesis of the plurality; each through his own performance draws the plurality together and in this act itself constitutes the group. The group in formation (or *groupe en fusion*) is thus an individual accomplishment. In the ontological sense of the word, there is no group *qua* ontological entity; there is only the omnipotent individual, and above him, nothing. The *groupe en fusion* results from the synthesizing or totalizing praxis of the individual man. It is from within, then, through the individual choice, that the plurality becomes unity. A group, or better still, a group in the process of formation, is nothing but a multiple and ubiquitous presence of each individual synthesis, hundreds of these syntheses upholding the group and embracing its totality in freedom.[2]

Clearly Sartre's approach is one which originates in the power of the *Cogito*, an example of the phenomenology of 'ascent' at its best. Yet I have doubts concerning this approach. What is hidden behind this phenomenology of ascent is the fact that Sartre in a Nietzschean way builds up the individual man as god of a social world and master of the universe. This position does not recognize that above the individual hangs a strange power. It is a power which he cannot shake off, but which guides him irresistibly, at times pierces his heart with a collective guilt, and often shows itself to be stronger than himself.

This power is dramatically illustrated in John Ford's masterful film, *The Informer*, where the man who betrayed the group was relentlessly pursued, despite the personal misgivings of the pursuers. "Whatever might have been the sympathy of the group members for Victor McLaglen in his role of the half-idiotic culprit, his condemnation to death had to stand, for the sake of the group. The decision could not be changed by and for an individual, or even by a few individuals who understood all the nuances of this muddled, bewildered life. The organization, a supra-individual entity,

---

[2] Jean-Paul Sartre, *Critique de la raison dialectique*, p. 384. For comment, see Desan, *The Marxism of Jean-Paul Sartre*.

had decided, and nothing could reverse that decision, for it belonged to a different dimension."[3]

In observing the individual by way of a phenomenology of 'descent,' the philosopher does not see him as a sovereign. On the contrary, he sees the individual as one pursued by forces and unavoidably caught, a Prometheus in chains. The fact is that the group holds the individual. To do this the group must have a power; and it has a power because it has an ontological status. The group decides and the individual acts within this decision.

What appears unintelligible to the individual may very well be intelligible to the group. What looks like destiny to the individual is merely the disposition of certain means toward an end that is visualized by the group. The group, whether existing in its elemental and natural way or in a man-made form, whether born for the pursuit of a natural aim or brought into existence for the achievement of some supernatural purpose, confronts a problematic situation and adopts a solution. This "choice" often appears as a mystery to the individual existent, but it compels him, nonetheless, as destiny.

The group manifests itself *in toto* and chooses a certain solution. The individual feels totally inadequate or even impotent until the group begins to move. I can very well visualize the conquest of the Bastille as the result of the group at work. The group was born before anyone's articulate awareness of it and before anyone's surge onto the Boulevarde, yet the group in its decision encompassed all and provoked a response in each one.

This praxis is a free decision, although no doubt motivated by the circumstances and not necessarily coinciding with one's individual preference. The group decision may force one into action, at times appearing "unreasonable" or detrimental to one's own interests. As the group takes a clear-cut shape, it may even seem to become a prison, and then of course the term 'destiny' comes to the fore. Yet the group is in fact merely acting in self-defense, as a group must, even though those actions be at the price of some of its unwilling "fragments."

'Descent' and Aspects of the Spiritual and Theological

We are now prepared for the application of the principles presented above to certain spiritual and theological considerations.

3 Wilfrid Desan, *The Marxism of Jean-Paul Sartre*, p. 296.

Before doing so, I would like to insist that I have no theological pretensions, but merely as a philosopher wish to provide by way of dialogue some remarks susceptible to discussion. The whole infrastructure of our thought needs reexamination. What I wish to say is merely the contribution of one conversant in the immense dialogue of minds in which philosophy fundamentally consists.

1. At a certain moment in time the Christian Church emerged as a group into the immense *totum genus humanum*. Others have pointed to this aspect of temporality—the church of Christ born in time. What I would like to stress is that this temporal appearance means that the Church itself cannot be the whole of humanity. The Church, on its own terms a *totum*, is a fragment within the context of the *totum genus humanum*. As fragment, it appears by way of succession.

The timing of the origin of this particular group is not clear, since its visible presence need not signify its birth. Indeed, St. Augustine wrote with great insight, "The reality which one today calls the Christian religion was present among the ancients; it has never ceased to exist since the origin of mankind, until Christ came into the flesh, the period when the true religion already existing began to call itself Christian." Augustine's words corroborate my contention that the group is there before the individual praxis and before any clearcut awareness of itself.

The Christian group, like every group in this process of formation, came together as a revolt, that is, it was a negation of a certain situation. In the very act of grouping, it was at the same time an assertion, the assertion of a belief in an Absolute. As such, the Christian group had been silently in the hearts of many before it could receive its explicit formulation through praxis. Christ was as much an incarnation of this will toward the Absolute that is present in the many as he was an incarnation of the Divine. The grouping together into the Church came, and comes, to the individual man from above. It seizes him because of an urge emanating from the totality itself: an urge which is in depth a drive for survival, in the case through eternal salvation. The individual Christian undoubtedly contributes to the Church, that is, he consciously co-responds to its conscious genesis. But as fragment of that particular totum or group, he was already involved in its pre-logical birth.

Eternal salvation is the absolute which has cemented the mobility of men into one. This oneness, or resulting *totum*, became visible with what St. Paul has called "the fullness of time," that is, at that moment of history when the internal movement of the group had reached its fullness and conveyed to its members the splendid opportunity for (external) praxis. One could equally well say that eternal salvation was chosen in and through the group, with the advent of Christ as a means of its achievement.

If one observes from the vantage point of the 'descent' from the periphery of the totum to its internal constituents, one notices, in addition to the cohesion of one just remarked, what might be called the mobility of the constituents. It is a case of mobility reaching mobility: the noetic mobility of the individual mind in its 'descent' reaching the spatial mobility of the constituents of the totality. If the consideration of immobility, oneness, or the *totum* is fruitful in insights, so too is the consideration of the fragment, or what might be termed the 'mobility diversified.' By 'mobility diversified' is understood the mobility of the fragments insofar as in this motion they betray their uniqueness.

In *The Planetary Man*, I wrote, "At the moment of (man's) entrance into the *totum—totum universum* and *totum humanum—* he is marked forever. His birth is his destiny."[4] The uniqueness of the individual's birth lies at the beginning of his journey through life. The motion of his life is the unique continuation of that which was his, and his alone, at his birth. The term *curriculum vitae* is a particularly apt one to signify the course or achievements of a life, since it points to its mobility: life is a journey, a "run."

Tertullian was well aware of this mobility when he defined the Christian not as something achieved and completed once and for all, but as one searching, journeying: *Christianus peregrinus est.* There is something exclusive, a never again, in this mobility of the individual. *Qua* individual existent he completes the totum to which he belongs, but he does so in a unique way. He is a *conditio-sine-qua-non* of the totum's being as it is. In our example, this would mean that each individual member makes the Church what it is.

2. Indeed, one sees in the *totum* Ecclesiae this same 'mobility diversified.' One immediate expression of this diversification is the hierarchical structure, which in its additive collectivity constitutes the *totum* that is the Church. In this light the bishop is seen to be

---

[4] Wilfrid Desan, *The Planetary Man* (Washington: Georgetown Univ. Press, 1961), I, 20.

no "better" than the priest, only different, the priest no "better" than the faithful, only filling a different role.

Collegiality, in this view, is seen to be the power belonging to the *totum qua totum*. Its implementation is clearly spread open in time and space, since the group itself is in its fundamental structure distributed over time and space. Space and time might be defined as that in which the group exists, that which distances its members, that which is between them, horizontally and vertically. Within the framework of the group, the need of balancing a diversity of functions is necessary; but this function, wherever or whenever it is exercised, does not in itself constitute the intrinsic worth of the individual. All the members are necessary, the great and small, for the attainment of the Absolute presumes an ontological inequality or diversity. "Upon the ontological basis of the unique and the unequal rests mutual completion, whether in succession or in horizontal simultaneity."[5]

3. The idea of 'mobility diversified' can lead us to a new approach toward freedom. I am inclined to believe that freedom can be found and defined in the unique mobility of a life. 'Mobility diversified' is freedom expressed. It is only in the form of 'descent' that one can discover within the *totum* this expression of freedom, since only in approaching the multiple from the outside can one discover the diverse and the unique. A diversity of decision or choice can be presumed only when many are present and only when the many act or behave diversely. Under the global span of the *totum* the many wander in different directions. These directions take many forms; they can cover the entire *curriculum vitae* or merely an act of agreement or disagreement, submission or revolt, teamwork or discord. Such behavior implies a 'mobility diversified,' and, when openly expressed, denotes a diversity of decision. Diversity of direction presumes diversity of decision, and the two undoubtedly presume freedom. Freedom presumed, I hasten to add, means neither freedom mathematically demonstrated nor freedom explained in all its noumenal texture. The freedom discovered here is merely the unique movement of individual men within the ambit of the *totum*.

A phenomenology of 'ascent' approaches freedom differently, as is well known, since in its perspective, freedom is merely the awareness of the possibles which the Self confronts and can make

5 *Ibid.*, p. 21.

its own. To put it synthetically but correctly, a phenomenology of 'ascent' discovers the multiple in man, while a phenomenology of 'descent' observes the multiple in the *totum* itself.

Mobility diversified, although implying exclusive uniqueness, does not mean independence. Men are diverse but they are not in-dependent. Individuals are dependent upon one another within the *totum*, whatever may be its size or shape. By way of 'descent' one can discover that what is born in time is dependent in space or, better still, that that which comes into the world through the Other (who was) can only survive through the Other (who is). The fragment lives its fragmentarity and through the space-time dimension is dependent upon the Other. This appears very clearly in the Christian group, where that which is born within the group can and will remain such only through the other. The collective is the preservative and must be so because of the relational structure of the constitutive parts of the *totum*.

This relational structure of the collective could be explored more deeply, but I would like instead to point to still another phenomenon which our phenomenology by way of 'descent' is able to discover. This phenomenon I call 'mobility restrained.' It has already been noted that the existence of a group implies the coalescence of its parts, resulting from the impact of an Absolute. The mobility discovered in the Christian *totum* is restrained by the Absolute of eternal salvation, eternal salvation through Christ. It is this which constitutes and holds together that group which calls itself "Christian."

By this I do not mean that the Christian totality is an homogeneous block and that each and every one of its members are equally affected by the conscious acceptance of a set of dogmas. Yet this acceptance is stronger than one is sometimes led to believe, and this strength comes down from the power of the *totum* to its members. It is the "we" that holds the "me" focussed upon the presence of the Absolute. Only those who have attempted to give up the Absolute have felt the formidable impact of the group as a withholding force.

This can be said of any group: the group has a power of and over its constituents that is unequalled. It constitutes a web that holds both the individual and the Absolute interlocked. The member of the group may go through a phase of doubt concerning the validity of the ideals propounded by the group, but in many cases the hold of the group over the individual will not loosen, or will do so only very slowly. The story of a conversion is in most cases, if not always, a painful one, of which only the candidate can narrate the sorrow. The same is true for the one who lapses and separates himself from the whole, from the group that is 'mobility restrained,' from the Absolute that the group alone faces with confidence.

This phenomenon is characteristic of a group still in its youth, or to use a Spenglerian metaphor, for a group still in its spring or summer. When the group goes through its autumn or winter, the 'mobility restrained' loses some of its internal force and spontaneous acceptance. 'Mobility restrained' may even become 'mobility enchained.' This is the phase of the group when commandments are multiplied, positive laws decreed, various checks and menaces promulgated, such as the Index or excommunication. When 'mobility restrained,' based upon a balance of group mandate with the personal conviction of its members, is on the wane, 'mobility enchained' comes to the rescue.

At this moment the danger is great that the mobility will not be restrained by its own convictions but enchained by fear. Fear is not faith. Far from protecting faith, fear in the long run kills it. If the phase of 'mobility enchained' is allowed to supplant the phase of 'mobility restrained,' a crisis is reached, for 'mobility enchained' conflicts with 'mobility diversified.'

'Mobility diversified' is an expression of freedom, of individual freedom, and of the unique journey of every man through life. The conflict between the freedom of the individual man and authoritarian excesses, or the conduct of the group by means of fear or ignorance, is a prelude to the agony of that group. Only through the respect for the existential unique of every man can the group survive. Only where the 'mobility diversified' is not crushed by the 'mobility enchained' does the group flourish as an organic and healthy totality, and can the *totum qua totum* attain its absolute.

Such, then, are some of the phenomena which a phenomenology of 'descent' is able to discover. They are not always in conflict with the results obtained by the Husserlian approach. But whether in conflict or not, they open a world which is not merely a creation of the individual self and which, as collective, overspans the multiple selves as the great "goodly frame" in which they move and are productive.

PART III

PHILOSOPHICAL PROBLEMS
IN RELIGIOUS RENEWAL

THE HUMAN PERSON AND GOD

by

MOTHER MARY CLARK, R.S.C.J.

Reflexion and research about the human person and God indicate a parallel with the Church's coming to self-consciousness and her efforts to clarify her mission to the modern world and to renew her modes of communication with contemporary man. This parallel is the universal urgency in man himself to know what he is so that he may direct cosmic evolution towards human ends or, if death proves to be his last horizon, be free from moral imperatives. The same research has revealed that man's religious experience of God's personal relations with him preceded the philosophical understanding of personhood developed by early Christian philosophers who meditated upon the scriptural references to Father, Son and Spirit as one God.

When in modern times reason was divorced from faith, the understanding of personhood as relatedness, primarily with divine persons, was gradually forgotten or suppressed in order to promote man's autonomy. Today, however, the descriptions of phenomenologists are once again bearing witness, albeit negatively, to the personal reality as essentially a related reality, and contemporary philosophers like MacMurray and Marcel explicitly emphasize the relationality rather than the rationality of man.

What is of vital importance in this to the Christian today is the effect that this intersubjective philosophy is having upon the theology of grace. Theologians are being pressed by philosophic thought, as it were, to recover and renew their understanding of man's participation in divine life by grace as participation in Trinitarian life. Christian philosophy cannot remain uninfluenced by this intellectual and affective ferment. In the practical order man's coming to consciousness of the dignity of his human vocation is a first step towards the fulfilment of his personal responsibility as a child of God to witness to the reality of a living God by his

89

own life of love for others. Thus man, especially the Christian, bears some responsibility for the atheism of our day. If the "universe is a vast thing in which we should be lost if it did not converge upon a person,"[1] there is nothing more necessary to search out than the human person who now holds the direction of the universe in his hands. In so serious a study as that of man, one may reject no insight, whether it be from classical philosophy, from the tradition of faith and reason, from the sciences or arts, or from contemporary complaints about the human condition.

This requires the ability to make a transition "from a mode of understanding that is descriptive, relational, interpersonal, historical-existential, to a mode of understanding that is definitive, explanatory, absolute, ontological."[2] Note, however, that description precedes definition. This is especially so when treating the human person who exists only as a unique, embodied being. It is, moreover, only through concrete actions that the person is knowable and perhaps then only from within, that is to say, when one is actually related to the person acting. If this is so, then the source material for this discussion of the human person and God will be, of course, sacred history.

Sacred History

In sacred history one discovers God inviting man to know him, to recognize him, and to acknowledge him. One sees God engaged in knowing man in the Hebraic sense of wholly relating himself to man, living with him, and walking ahead of him or with him, as now he is not far from any of us.[3]

The human person emerged from the events of this sacred history —Exodus, Sinai, Alliance, Code—with religious responsibility acquired through a maturing process of community life with God who introduced himself to Moses in the Burning Bush as Yahweh and as the God of the community founded by Abraham. This name gives a major clue to what being a person means, that is, someone correlative with community. What did the Jews understand by Yahweh, which literally means: I am who I am? The Rev. John

1 P. Teilhard de Chardin, S.J., *Letters from a Traveller* (New York: Harper, 1962), p. 216.
2 J. C. Murray, S.J., *The Problem of God* (New Haven: Yale University Press, 1964), p. 46.
3 Acts 17:27.

Courtney Murray thinks that this name was received into the primitive mentality of the Hebrew people as neither a metaphysical nor a cosmological, but a personal message telling them of his role as the Power of their father's community, the community he had created. If the meaning of the name God called himself ('ehyeh) is this: "I shall be there with you in power," it is echoed on the eve of Judah's restoration: "Therefore my people shall know my name; therefore in that day they shall know that it is I who says: 'Here I am'."[4]

Understanding Yahweh as "I shall be there as 'who I am' shall I be there," theology will translate this personal experience of God's communication to Moses into an explanation of the divine being as present to man or immanent, as different from man or transcendent, and as accessible to man as transparent power through his actions and visitations to his people or omnipotent. Fully and concretely, Yahweh's name signifies his unchanging fidelity to his promise of presence with his people. It is with regard to this promise that we are to understand Malachi's prophecy, "I (am) Yahweh; I do not change."[5]

Classical Philosophy

That emergence of certain Asian tribes into a community led by God was the first step in the development of human personhood in history. But the first philosophical precision concerning the person was made by the Greek Fathers of the Church in their reflexion upon the trinity of Persons in God. The early Church had been concerned with the likeness of Son and Spirit to the Father, stressing their consubstantiality by reason of the threat and sometimes the teaching of subordinationism. Their problem was unity rather than trinity, nature rather than person.

In the history of man's reflexion upon man one finds a certain parallel. The first philosophical thinking was concerned with the likeness of man to man, that is, with the universal discoverable in the particular or with the common nature of all men, whether this commonness was attributed to participation in a transcendent form or to an immanent substantial form. The period of concentration upon nature lasted much longer in philosophy than in theology. This is reflected in the literature of the world. Until very recently

4 Is. 52:6.
5 Mal. 3:6.

the literary writings of all countries featured *types* of people rather than unique individuals. If, as in *Pilgrim's Progress,* the allegory was not always explicit, it was implicitly there nonetheless as each reader recognized by praising the author for deftly holding the mirror to human nature. There remained the reader's unexpressed hope that self-knowledge would come by seeing human nature refracted in a myriad of fictional or historical characters which the 19th century science of psychology later built upon in its development of typology.

Yet, as early as the third Christian century, theologians realized that none of the Divine Persons could remain divine while lacking anything in respect to the Divine Substance. Each Divine Person would have to be unique by its mode of existing, a mode which they declared constituted by "origin" (the Unbegotten, the Begotten, the Procession). Later, theologians of the Middle Ages suggested that the manner in which each Person acts toward the other or is present to the other constitutes each unique personhood. Thus the personal relation is action. The second Person is Son to the Father, a real relation which also includes the "origin" because this Son-reality as personal is intersubjective. These medievals, unlike the Greek Fathers, recognized "action" as the expression of a spiritual being's concrete wholeness, a synthesis of thought and love, belonging to the "I" by means of the nature.

In the real order, the order of action, the person has primacy. This allows us to suggest that in a profound sense all persons are constituted by interpersonal relations. Here we should reflect that not even the Absolute is unrelated. Without personal relations the Absolute would not be infinite perfection. Insofar as a person is an end and never a means, a person is an absolute in the sense that its dignity is intrinsic, not depending upon its usefulness and desirability as is the way with things. In this way a human person, though finite and never the final point of reference, nevertheless participates in the absolute value of infinite Being.

Yet is there no opposition between an absolute which is supposedly *ad se* and a subject who in being *ad alium* must depend on others to be itself? Apparently this is a logical contradiction and not a real one. Both aspects are reconciled in that existent whose personal reality is so inter-subjective that in order to be "for himself" he is required to be "for others." Only action in harmony with this intersubjective structure can succeed in synthesizing the absolute aspects and the relative aspects of the human personality, because personal substance and personal relation are not exterior to each other. That is why every action signifies beyond its ostensible target the personal attitude of the agent, his attitude towards others. Thus, the actions of persons invariably unite them or divide them from others; personal actualization is never accomplished in solitude. Love, as we learn from St. Augustine, is at the origin of the Word from the Unbegotten Father and love also unites Father and Son. Love is the proper attitude between persons because it respects their "wholeness." Parts are united by a necessity, while "wholes" are united by a free tie which they originate.

St. Thomas, unlike the Greek and many medieval theologians, refused to admit that the Divine Persons were constituted as persons by the passive side of their relation to one another, that is, by their origin. He pioneered in teaching that "origin" cannot constitute a person; generation by the Father is not a person but a "way towards it." If one says that "the name person signifies relation,"[6] it is the internal relation of the essence which diversifies it.[7] The divine acts which are productive of the Persons in the Trinity are said to be the reason and cause for the procession of creatures. But since creation as utterly free was an uncaused act, it is as final cause that one speaks of the production of Persons as the reason for creation. The person then becomes the key which unlocks the meaning of the universe.

St. Thomas and St. Bonaventure agree in asserting that the Divine Persons are really distinguished from one another by their origin and constituted as persons by their relations.[8] Love is at the root of the two processions because a Personal Agent acts through love, and action originates and ends in a person. But love is incomplete when not reciprocated and therefore the Divine Persons are not really distinguished from one another without their appropriate response to the love which originates each one. This love-response constitutes a relation which in God is a person identical with the divine essence. Likewise, although all men share, if not a numerically identical essence, at least a common human one, they are really distinct from one another as persons. Although God's personal love

---

[6] Thomas Aquinas, *Summa Theologica*, I, q. 29, a. 4.
[7] Thomas Aquinas, *De Potentia*, q. 8, a. 3, ad 7; *Summa Theologica*, I, q. 40, a. 4.
[8] A. Malet, *Personne at Amour* (Paris, Vrin, 1956); cf. A. Krempel, *La doctrine de la relation dans St. Thomas* (Paris: Vrin, 1952).

for each can be said to be the ontological root of this real distinction, persons are constituted, can we not say, as uniquely distinct from one another by each one's love-response to God?

Now if it is true that man is the only being who is constituted by a personal relation to God, let us admit that a personal relation is incomplete without reciprocity. The affective activity of the human person is therefore of major and not minor importance. Instead of being relegated to the realm of the irrational, man's affectivity should be recognized as fundamental for his personal well-being. It is inaccurate then to characterize man solely by his intellectual life. "Intellectual" may specifically qualify the nature by which man acts, but it remains an inadequate label for the human person. A certain proof of this is the fact that only one person is needed to actualize intellectual life whereas the life of love requires other persons and thereby better qualifies personal existence which is existence in community.

There is a certain sign that man is on the right road to fulfilment, and that sign is the indefinable but the inescapable joy that friendship brings. This joy is not the cause of friendship but a material, dispositive cause which serves to allure one to the love of the good for itself, just as falling-in-love is the ordinary natural mechanism which opens persons to a more spiritual relationship which is the ground for the fidelity of married life.[9] The joy of friendship is a certain natural sign that one is in close contact with the human good or end. When one says that persons are ends and not means, thereby possessing absolute value which invites one's respect, this indeed signifies that finite persons participate not merely in being-as-such but in personal-being: the essence of the good. That is why love for persons is always a love for the good and consequently it is our good.[10]

The medieval appreciation of personhood as relatedness, and primarily as relatedness with the Divine Persons, involved the acceptance of man's metaphysical situation. Later centuries, with their increasing emphasis on scientism, deny precisely that metaphysical situation by an appeal to man's apparently inexhaustible autonomy. The results are all too apparent in the modern world, whether it be the western world of individualistic self-sufficiency or the communist world of collective anti-personalism.

9 St. Thomas Aquinas, *Summa Theologica*, II-II, q. 27, a. 4; q. 23, a. 6.
10 *Ibid.*, I, q. 6, aa. 2 & 3.

Existential Phenomenology

Now intrepid thinkers like Jaspers, MacMurray, Nédoncelle and Marcel are casting exciting lights upon the horizon. For example, there is Marcel's earliest description, in the play *The Just Man*, of fidelity as a problem bound up with self-betrayal. In it we find that the man of fidelity lives in a personal universe, a spiritual atmosphere; it is the world of a promise-keeper or one faithful to his word in the midst of changing conditions and changing moods.

In another play Marcel shows us the home of Christiane and Laurent where each person is concerned only with himself; there is an absence of any inner unity in this "Broken World." But through the faithful prayers of the monk Jacques for Christiane, for whom he feels responsible, Christiane attains to a moment of truth when she is strengthened to renew the sacred bond with her husband Laurent. Once again, fidelity becomes creative of a higher unity when persons transcend their broken world by becoming really present to each other through the permanence of their promise. Marcel always makes one see the fraternal man as being enriched by everything which enriches his brother. When he describes "hope" he shows it, not in the usual sense of hoping for something for oneself, but as a hope which is creative of one's fellowman because it transforms him and enables him to grow. The transfigured man is the related man.

By far the greater number of literary artists, however, have pictured the unrelated man today in his phenomenon of self-alienation. Ibsen's Peer Gynt, Beckett's tramps waiting for Godot, Camus' Judge-penitent—all manifest the sickly traits of "the Outsider." Probing to the heart of the Outsider's malaise, phenomenologists, dramatists, and novelists have discovered in terms all can understand the reality of anguish. Some see it arising from an unbearable responsibility for the creation of values now that God's death has left values ungrounded. Others see it arising from the decision not to choose, from the misery of living superficially or the impossibility of dedicating one's self to one's work. But if anguish expresses dissatisfaction, it also implies a feeling of guilt because a man is not what he somehow feels called to be. This suggests that things can indeed be different, thereby witnessing to a deep conviction of human freedom. It is the very freedom of the person which seems to account for the breach in the human person, its non-coincidence, or the gap which exists between the self and the actuality of being for which it thirsts. In this respect anguish may well be in some minimal form a "natural" undercurrent of personal development. Nevertheless, freedom is both man's capacity for steadily closing the gap and his sole responsibility.

Person and Relation

It was noted that there is a certain confirmation from above that the human anguish depicted in current literature is rooted in some basic frustration of man's being. Even without this suggestion, which came from Faith seeking understanding, some contemporary philosophers have gone beyond phenomenology to express the significance of certain human experiences as indicating that man is fundamentally himself in and through personal relationships. John MacMurray states that the "self exists only in dynamic relation with the other,"[11] citing as evidence the human infant adapted by birth to a complete dependence upon a human being. He shows that all the early manifestations of personal mutuality as the human milieu can be interpreted to indicate that personal existence is not the individual but two persons in personal relation. To be, for man, means to be open to the other so that the person becomes himself in relation to the other. What above all becomes clear here is that personal experience described by the phenomenologists and expressed in the ordinary words of fidelity, hope, love, hatred, fear, anxiety, and anguish require the positing of an interpersonal reality, a personal mutuality.

It is MacMurray's conviction that the childish experience of dependence upon a personal other—of openness in love and confidence—finds its normal and real expression in religion. The family experience as a common one accounts then for the universality of religion. Fully developed, the idea of a permanent, personal Other, always present, is the idea of God. If love is the motive of this personal relationship, then indeed religion develops into the celebration of communion, the fellowship of all in God.

What then is the consensus of contemporary philosophers about man today? "Man is the being who is related to God," says Karl Jaspers;[12] "Man exists only by relation to God," Guardini[13] tells us; Berdyaev insists that "to consider man is already to consider

11 MacMurray, *Persons in Relation* (New York: Harper, 1961), p. 17.
12 K. Jaspers, *Introduction a la Philosophie* (Paris: Plon, 1952), p. 85.
13 R. Guardini, *La Puissance* (Paris: Seuil, 1954), p. 115.

God";[14] and one would expect Kierkegaard to say: "To lack God is to lack myself."[15]

In addition to these philosophical witnesses there is the testimony of the theologians that the Divine Persons are established from and through a love relationship and that they have made man to their image. Hence, it is not enough to say that what constitutes a human person is a spiritual nature (an *id quo*) and the subsistence of that nature (an *id quod*), for the existential wholeness and concrete uniqueness of each person requires the addition to its mode of existing of that which qualifies it as unique, namely, the individual love relationship that grounds its special creation by God.

Ontology of Love and Divine Presence

The consensus among formal and informal philosophical writers that the person is deeply, ontologically relational does then find confirmation in the theological understanding of the Trinity and in the scriptural history of God's relations with his chosen people and of the Son's relations with their descendants. Nevertheless, it does not find in the theology of grace what might be called a satisfactory presentation of the human person's relations with God as person, that is, as Father, Son, and Holy Spirit.

In the theological discussion of nature's orientation to grace as nature's fulfilment, there has been emphasis upon the mere absence of any natural contradiction to man's reception of grace. In this purely negative way some have interpreted man's "obediential potency" as a mere non-interference on man's part with the positive supernatural reality offered by God. Yet, if it is true that a longing for the Absolute Being is, as Maréchal teaches, fundamentally though not explicitly, present in every spiritual act as the a priori condition of every existential judgment, man can by consciously formulating this desire become aware of a profound dimension of the depths of his spiritual being—its direction towards God. If this orientation is affirmed implicitly in every act of his spirit, it is making man what he experiences himself to be—a longing for Totality.

The admittedly necessary precaution of emphasizing the gratuitousness of grace has resulted, as Karl Rahner points out, in regarding grace as a mere supernatural structure leaving the ground floor

---

14 N. Berdyaev, *Cinq meditations sur l'esprit* (Paris: Aubier, 1956), p. 28.
15 S. Kierkegaard, *Traité du désespoir* (Paris: Gallimard, 1949), p. 106.

of nature untouched. Yet modern man has learned to think existentially in the 20th century and is interested, not in analysis, but in the synthesis which the human person constitutes. Man's deep longing for totality has inspired his search for knowledge so that he has come to reject any partial view as monstrous. The synthesis he needs must include all that can be known about the full reality of man, from biology, anthropology, chemistry, physics, psychology, psychiatry, sociology, philosophy past and present, and from theology or revelation. He rightly feels that if chemicals can alter human action, existence, and personality, why should not grace if it is a reality? If grace does affect human existence, must it not radically and totally affect the person? And if grace is a participation in divine existence, must it not open to man that relation-structure which is wholeness of being? Unlike God, those to whom man relates are outside his own natural being; his longing for wholeness cannot be fulfilled from within.

But if grace affects man ontologically—and the human person has been accurately described by phenomenologists and understood by philosophers—then new relationships are established within those to whom Emmanuel comes. In the past almost exclusive attention has been paid to created rather than uncreated grace in man. Hence, the person has tended to think of himself as supernaturally "qualified" by grace, rather than as one who becomes the host of the Spirit whom the Father and Son breathe forth and whose love generates new sons of God into Trinitarian life. The presence of "God with us" constitutes not only the change effected by created grace, a new life-quality, but more precisely that in which this life consists: an intimate relation to the three persons of the Trinity and a participation in their relation to one another.

The long maturation of the human mind and emergence of the human person through history by his self-differentiation from the cosmos, his internalization of the cosmos, and his self-transcendence with his present feeling of cosmic responsibility have culminated in a self-consciousness arousing anguish or despair. Man's reflections upon the human condition, refusing to bracket anything *real*, have converged in the almost universal conviction that there is need to restore, purify, and strengthen man's relations, not primarily with the cosmos, but with other persons. The development of the Apollonian aspects in the human being has outstripped that of the Dionysian forces which, becoming alienated from truth, separated themselves and left to their destructive devices the abandoned, darkened, and anguished human reality. These modern minds become self-conscious, are ready to admit that there is a more serious, basic, and universal problem than that of the underdeveloped nations. This is the problem of the underdeveloped person. Personal immaturity may very well be the greatest threat to world security today. Love must begin, although not end, at home; and the home where love grows is the "we" of the "between" of persons.

Hence, those for whom synthesis has become almost instinctive and who believe that Christ became incarnate to redeem man by bringing him to know God with an understanding heart and a loving knowledge which relates man totally to God (epignosis) are pressing theologians. These are being asked to develop the dogmas and morality of the Church along lines which will restore and renew the interpersonal relationships which are to be found in the scriptural history of God's dealing with man. If all world progresss depends upon personal progress, there is nothing more called for today than a clear, public theology of grace that heals and uplifts man in his love-relationships. Teilhard de Chardin's synthesis of science and revelation had no other purpose than to make manifest to all that Christ's salvation-history is indeed world-history. Karl Rahner's investigations of uncreated grace can be viewed as a certain response to modern man's call for personal communication with God with its inevitable fruit: communion with others. Thus he writes:

> If (as Pius XII says) grace and glory are two stages of the one process of divinization and, as classical theology has always held, in glory God communicates himself to the supernaturally elevated created spirit in a communication which is not the *efficient* causal creation of a creaturely quality or entity distinct from God, but the quasi-formal causal communication of God himself, then this can also be applied to *grace* much more explicitly than it commonly has been in theology up till now. "Uncreated grace" will then no longer be regarded as merely the consequence of the creation of 'infused' grace, constituting the state of grace, as a "physical accident," but rather as the very essence of grace (which also explains much better how grace can strictly be a mystery, for a purely created entity as such can never be an absolute mystery). God communicates himself to man in his own reality. That is the mystery and the fullness of grace. From this the bridge to the mystery of the Incarnation and the Trinity is easier to find.[16]

16 K. Rahner, *Nature and Grace* (New York: Sheed and Ward, 1964), p. 125.

As Schillebeeckx has seen,[17] although nature does not require Christ, Christ requires nature to carry out his plan to dwell among us, to restore Emmanuel, to communicate with all men and bring all into unity. The cosmos has not evolved into a Christian cosmos, true; but Christ by the incarnational principle has made this world his milieu. When through Christ man is completed by grace, he becomes not only a capacity to respond freely and with love to God and to others as intrinsically valuable or absolute, but an actual ability to respond. When man experiences his engraced personality on this level of love for the other, he becomes aware of himself as one restored to himself and radically renewed. The Church today is trying to communicate to the whole world this consciousness of herself as the presence of Charity, as the heart of God in the midst of men. This communication depends, of course, upon the presence of authentic Christians whose ability to respond to God makes them responsive to the needs of men and enables the future of the universe to be safely entrusted to their responsibility. In this sense the emergence of the person through history, universal history which includes both the sacred and the profane, comes full circle: man is no longer in the universe, the universe is within man.

When we return to the experience of being as the phenomenologists of alienation and the philosophers of intersubjectivity have stimulated us to see it, we perceive that the phenomena described point infallibly to the profound significance of the ontology of love. In the evolving, proceeding, converging and changing world man seems intended to find security not in the stability of immutable substance but rather in the dynamism of BEING or LOVE which is, after all, the metaphysical reality underlying the names of God revealed by the faithful Yahweh and the faithful Son. This reality that is love is active yet abiding, free yet urgent—it builds the homes and hearths of earth and is the sole maker of the mansions of heaven.

This being that is love is precisely what grace divinizes. Yet here one must note that the human person is an embodied spirit, and that his personal actions are corporeal, historical, and social. Moreover, the grace that man receives, as in direct conformity with the Incarnate Son, a Spirit made flesh, is an incarnational grace. It

---

[17] E. Schillebeeckx, *Christ the Sacrament of the Encounter with God* (New York: Sheed and Ward, 1963).

brings with it the Father's mandate which then becomes man's mission to incarnate the Father's love for man, to manifest it, publicize it, and dramatize it by giving it authentic corporeal, historical, and social dimensions. Like the Son, the Christian is called to incarnate that love, to give it flesh and blood, so that it can visibly serve, save, and sometimes die for others. Christianity may well be, as Teilhard de Chardin has said, the phylum of love in the world. If so, to understand this world, one is in need of both faith and reason, just as to be Christian one needs both nature and grace, while to be oneself he needs both the human person and God.

The Person and Action

Because the Christian has not borne witness to the Divine Indwelling we may well be assisting at a deathbed scene, the end of the post-modern period marked by the death of man, the inevitable consequence of believing the Nietzschean myth of the death of God. What this sick world is crying out for is the infallible witness of living men to awaken godless men to the reality of the living God.

Christian philosophy can contribute in its way to religious renewal and serve the cause of Christian unity so dear to the heart of John XXIII by reflexion upon the human person as a "religious being" and upon the Christian person as "Spirit": openness to God; personality as freedom, consciousness, and love; and what St. Paul calls the "pneumatic man" or more usually the "spiritual man." To define the human person as a created spirit is to say that it is openness to infinite being; and this is to say that it cannot be defined because it cannot be confined. The supernatural elevation of man is the absolute (although unmerited) fulfilment of this being. But what Karl Rahner accents is that in the historical order grace has been offered to all men and that there will be signs of this in man's experience of himself, which experience includes either the presence or the absence of God.

Reflexion upon the consciousness of the human subject, stimulated by contemporary directions in philosophy, delivers to man an unobjective knowledge of his own personal reality and of the personal reality of the infinite creating origin of being, insofar as his consciousness contains a free decision or attitude towards God as the horizon of every choice whereby man disposes of himself. This self-possession, verified in choice, distinguishes the personal act from the act of nature and actualizes man as person. When man's choice arises not only from his personal center but reaches another personal center on behalf of that other we have self-gift which is the authentic sign of man's self-possession as personal responsibility.

As a person man is a response in knowledge, love, and freedom to the love of God which is profoundly present in the heart of every real situation and event. Things and natures react but a person responds totally to reality by thought, choice, feeling, and action. In so doing man closes the gap between person and nature; but, insofar as he cannot make this response total, man is deprived of the integrity God willed him to have, originally, and now redemptively.

Thus, if "responsibility" best characterizes the human person because it indicates both the incommunicability which denotes the person as the ultimate source of his actions and the communicability which denotes community as the natural human milieu, and if man's ability to make a response of love to God is the result of grace, then it would seem best to think of the person as *actualization* of the human vocation. For the human vocation includes both nature and the self, as well as the "supernatural existential." Awareness of this vocation brings a full awareness of human dignity. The Father's notional or personal love for the Son terminates creatively in the human person who is then constituted in personhood as the divine Son was, that is, in being radically for the Father. As Augustine expressed it long ago: Thou hast made us for Thyself (*ad te*). When man, by the power of created grace which conforms him to the Son, ratifies this radical orientation towards the Father, the Spirit of Love or uncreated grace comes to dwell within all man's personal actions, which then can create, save, and sanctify by the power of this Love which abides in him.

Hence, in some ineffable way the concrete vocation of man is trinitarian, a call by created grace, offered to all men, to share in the generation of the Son with the Father, responding with the Son to the Father, and together with Father and Son breathing forth the Spirit. This vocation is the highest horizon of man's dignity and yet belongs to every man. But if this is a great mystery, a great mystery also, as Gabriel Marcel has emphasized, is the existence of unique human persons, for the creation of persons into human life and their elevation into trinitarian life are but two moments of one Love. Because divine love is the human person's origin and vocation, reason can never adequately comprehend the human person.

His origin in God and his openness to God will keep the human person undefined.

The above has attempted to indicate why the contemporary drive to discuss and dramatize, to explore and analyze the human person requires a return to the religious experience of man's call by the Living God. This in turn requires a return to the tradition of faith seeking understanding. But if the bible is history and if history has helped to constitute mankind, then the anguish experienced by contemporary man is not merely the result of the absence of God but is the ontological pain arising from the privation of God. It is privation rather than absence which causes physical pain. To interpret the modern consciousness in this way which does justice to the dimension of history and to the psychology of repression will require Christian philosophers; but to renew the experience of God in the daily lives of contemporary men requires reawakened Christians who love incarnationally. The Living God today is brought to presence by those who image him as his Son did in his love for every man. To be recognized as living by twentieth-century man, God needs living Christians. As St. John said (3, 13-18): "Remember that we have changed over from death to life, in loving the brethren as we do, whereas, if a man is without love, he holds fast by death."[18] There is need for living men, alive with love, to awaken men to recognize the living God. Then they will be able to say with the Psalmist: "The Lord stood by me, and brought me out into freedom again: his great love befriended me."[19] To people the world with loving men whose love leads to that understanding which is creative of true community—this is the purpose of the call of John XXIII to Christian renewal. To respond to this call the human person must innovate or renew the dogmas of his Faith and the conclusions of Christian philosophy by incarnating them anew in his personal and social action. When he did this, he is truly imaging God's incarnate Son and fulfilling his total responsibility.

Conclusion

A future Christian philosophy of the human person must do justice to the totality of man's self-consciousness. This includes at least a renewed sense of himself as radical responsibility by which

18 John, Ep. 3:13-18.
19 Ps. 17:19-20.

he shares, as it were, in divine freedom mingled with that very human quality of perfectibility. Because of man's obediential potency, his is indeed an infinite perfectibility; but the burden of his human dignity can be borne if he does not attempt to bear it alone. Thus, the knowledge that personal being at its best is being-with-others should guide his life toward friendship, so that he likewise may enkindle others to emerge from individualism or collectivism into personal community wherein a man receives the courage *to-be-himself*, the courage *to-love*.

FREEDOM AND CHRISTIAN PHILOSOPHY

by

REVEREND L.-B. GEIGER, O.P.

Notions of Freedom

The theme of the relationship between man and God concerned man's mind long before it achieved a state of reflection sufficient to formulate this relationship clearly and express it intelligibly. Though this theme first appeared in mythology, its forms of expression were ignored for a long time by philosophers precisely because philosophy had been born in Greece with the intention of rising above the level of mythology. Nevertheless there was the myth of Prometheus, the jealousy of the gods, and the justice of fate which forces anyone back into the common lot who seeks to elevate himself above this level. Finally there was the theme of *hybris* which constitutes a powerful temptation as fatal as a poison causing the loss of reason, and plunging the imbiber blindly into enterprises in which he will be destroyed as certainly as the son of Atreus, plagued by his cruel but relentless fate.

This is not the place to consider in detail either the content or the significance of these myths or others which have flowed from them. But in them one sees clearly that:

(1) the rational creature is conscious of the existence of limits within which he feels himself enclosed or ensnared;

(2) by the very same token he is also conscious of the presence within himself of a certain force which is restrained by these limits and at the same time extends itself to break forth beyond them, as if there existed a natural conflict between the development for which the human being feels himself destined and the condition of the universe in which he finds himself placed; and

(3) in these myths and in much later periods this conflict, instead

105

of being experienced, understood, and formulated in technical terms, was understood as man's encounter with the gods, or more generally, with the world of the divine.

The progress of man thus appeared in its ensemble as an undertaking which is at once both necessary and fatal. It is necessary since it is based upon an interior force which constitutes a sort of irresistible temptation. It is fatal because based upon a dangerous, even sacrilegious, undertaking which leads man to struggle with powerful forces whose resources he neither understands nor comprehends, but whose jealousy and spirit of vengeance he thinks he knows.

Such a situation is understandable on the supposition that the human being finds himself in the presence of a world of gods upon whom he does not depend in his very being. This would be a world of divinities identical to those of all peoples who know nothing of creation properly so called. In this supposition the world of the gods would be perhaps a more perfect and happier one, but it could only be juxtaposed to the universe of men. One could easily understand that these gods, if they were not already the product of human anger, would desire to preserve the realm and the prerogatives which distinguish them from men, that is, to prevent any presumptuous undertaking which would wrest their exclusive enjoyment from them. Accordingly these gods would have to be moved in a completely natural manner, as would any social class which seeks to distinguish itself from inferior classes by a desire to possess exclusively the powers and the knowledge which give them their specific character.

As long as man accepts such a view of things, he would consider himself to be in the tragic position of being necessarily driven to scale Olympus. A relentless force would counsel him to break forth from the situation which is his, to free himself from the limits which encompass his knowledge and from the shackles which prevent him from enjoying the good of life to the degree that he desires. He would be torn between, on the one hand, the thirst which is part of his very being and, on the other hand, the limitations against which he struggles. Success in pushing back such limits would give him the impression of having reached out far beyond his measure, and leave him with the feeling of having undertaken a more or less sacrilegious venture.

One of the central affirmations of the Christian faith, inherited from the Old Testament, is that the true God created heaven and earth and all that they contain with such good pleasure that he looked upon each of his works as good, even as very good. Man, for his part, was not haphazardly formed, but made by God himself to his image and likeness. He was entrusted to rule the entire universe and commanded to go forth, to multiply, and to inhabit the earth.

When the apostles went forth to preach the good news to the pagan world, they took care to stress the degree to which the doctrine which they announced in the name of Jesus Christ marked men's liberation from all the powers, elements, and fate which weighed so heavily upon the conscience of the hellenistic world. "You are citizens of the city of the saints, you are of the house of God," sons of God and coheirs with Christ. The new doctrine was received with joy. In fact, it gave the first Christians the consciousness of being at last free of all the forms of slavery in which, not only the worship of the gods, but the doctrine of the philosophers had held them.

Within the last century one of the most constant reproaches voiced against religion in general and Christian thought in particular is precisely that it is an enemy of man's true freedom. For this reason, atheism itself no longer takes exception to this or that point in the proofs of the existence of God. Instead, it bases itself upon the simple evidence of men's freedom in order to draw from it the conclusion that one must choose either man and his freedom, or God. If God exists, man cannot be free. But man is free; and from all the evidence concerning the constituents of his most authentic being, he must be free and wishes to be so. Thus God does not and cannot exist.

In fact, even the idea of God must be suppressed to render possible authentic human existence. Mechanistic determinism thought itself able to found the negation of God upon the demonstration of the incompatibility, on the one hand, of divine action and human liberty to interrupt or simply to modify the rigorous interlocking of causes and effects and, on the other hand, of the laws which govern their succession. In opposition to this position, a large part of modern and contemporary philosophy has considered it necessary to deny the existence and the possibility of God in order to remain faithful to the most evident reality: human freedom. Hence, today man finds himself once again in the presence of an antinomy between men's liberation and religion. It is as if the very word religion could be taken only according to one of its etymological meanings to signify bond with all that the word could suggest of restraint or rein, and consequently of a principle antagonistic to the zeal for freedom.

It is not the purpose of this paper to treat in its entirety or in its various aspects the problem of the relationship between religion and the irresistible desire of humanity to contribute to the process of evolution by efforts aimed at conquering or avoiding limitations. For the mass of humanity space exploration is a most expressive symbol of this. Tentative analogies can be found in all the domains of human activities, technical and artistic, and in scientific as well as psychological or anthropological theories.

This paper limits itself to the more precise and certainly more difficult problems of human freedom properly so called. Without a doubt, the process of liberation must lead to greater liberty. But one can conceive the possibility, even the necessity, of a sustained effort for liberation which is not founded on a formal claim for interior liberty, and especially for liberty as conceived by a large part of philosophy. Moreover certain advocates of liberation have refused the privilege of true liberty or freedom to the individual, seeing in it a vestige of bourgeois and individualistic philosophy which, guided by a sense of history, they feel must give way to truly anonymous and superhuman force.

Within the general problem of the liberation of man, that of freedom constitutes a particular question with its own proper characteristics. To the general notion of opposition to limits or to exterior constraint, it adds the idea of a profound liberation of man from all which could influence him in any way whatsoever. Indeed, this freedom must be considered not as a force launched against the universe which impedes it, but rather as a force whose source is capable of giving meaning to its activity and to the effects which it produces.

The precise problem of freedom as it actually presents itself to Christian philosophy will be the object of the following reflections. They will show:

(1) how and why a certain interpretation and claim for freedom leads a part of contemporary thought to atheism;

(2) how, on the contrary, reflection on this same freedom, and its importance for a sane understanding of man, leads other contemporary thinkers to discover there the need for a re-

ligious attitude, without which freedom would cease to be what it truly is; and

(3) how to draw out from this twofold exposition the conclusions which follow for a Christian philosophy of freedom and its relationship with God.

Freedom: a Foundation for Atheism

The establishing of freedom as a base of atheism is part of a movement which dates from the past and of which Feuerbach is increasingly given the honor of being the initiator. Recent works such as those of Arvon caution against oversimplifying the thought of this philosopher. However, he clearly held that a human being cannot find himself fully unless he leaves behind him the alienation in which he abdicated his best qualities to a God of his own making. Man gave up the personal pursuit of an ideal of humanity, and did this for a being existing only in his imagination. It is important, therefore, to denounce the alienation, even to annul it, and then to liquidate this God who exists only in one's ignorance.

This theory of alienation was used in the general Marxist social doctrines of class struggle and of the development of humanity. This would be fully reconciled with itself once all causes of the distinction and opposition of human beings had been eliminated by the communist society. Spread abroad amongst the most diverse levels of society, this theory has taken hold among all peoples and continents where Marxist influence has managed to infiltrate. By it, the idea of an ineluctable conflict between the desire to progress and the true freedom of man, on the one hand, and religion, on the other hand, has come to be accepted as evidence by a growing segment of humanity, educated or not.

The theme of alienation, at least in Marxism, remains necessarily related to an understanding of history as unable to be influenced by any individual. In Marxism, it is not formally men's liberty which is at issue and which opposes him to God, but man's liberation precisely with reference to God and all that his faith in God implies. Marxism looks at the evolution of humanity and the realization of its true end, rather than at the conditions of true liberty.

Sartre's position is quite different. He places himself primarily on the side of the individual and emphasizes liberty before any other aspect of the real. According to him, a philosophy such as that of

Heidegger, which does not take this as its point of departure, must condemn itself never to find it. Whatever their differences may be, the philosophies of existence along with the phenomenologists and against Cartesians and rationalists have insisted that it is the opening to the world which is first given and from which one must start, if he does not wish to be weighed down by mere abstractions. Men are not, first of all, isolated substances which must search to open themselves to the world. Initially and by reason of the intentional structure of conscience they are present, or even more exactly, presence to the world.

For Sartre such a point of departure is pregnant with danger. Is one not falling back into philosophies of being, indeed into the realism and all its consequences over which contemporary thought has triumphed? The point of departure of the philosophies of existence appears to be beyond doubt. If one adopts this and does not wish to abandon the evident liberty of conscience which is the typical mode of being of conscience, one is bound to conclude that conscience does not rise up before a given world with its diverse given meanings which can be read as one reads a book. For Sartre, consciousness is born like a disease or decompression of being. It is a pure initiative filled with meaning by itself and therefore only for itself. On the basis of this first step, the world itself emerges into existence with meaning which it has only by me and for me.

It is not necessary to insist on the extreme consequences with which Sartre has been obliged to invest his principles, namely:

(1) that consciousness should not have any other title than nothing ("néant") in order to avoid everything which might contaminate the pure development of liberty as he conceives it;

(2) that every objective value has to be rejected, on the pretext that such objective values would dominate my decision from without; and

(3) that God must be rejected because the idea of creation, applied to liberty, is contradictory: a free being, by definition, being in opposition to its creator from the very moment in which he is free and poses an act of liberty.

The important facts to be emphasized here are two. First, in the philosophy of Sartre neither liberty nor liberation are simply an operation or activity brought about by a human being, who for his part is a being determined by his nature. A being which is able to pose a single free act must be fully free in its very being. He has, therefore, neither nature nor being, but only nothing. In this lies the novelty of his thought, in opposition to the atheism or anti-theism of the Greeks and moderns.

Secondly, only by reason of his interpretation of liberty does the being of man logically involve the absolute rejection of all objective values and dependence on God. Sartre can be shown to stand in a long tradition which, under the guise of the liberty of the human conscience, thinks almost exclusively in physical images and terms. Liberty is described as an energy or a power to launch something, including to launch the meaning of launching itself. Liberty, then, is simply the point of origin, and this origin must necessarily be a pure one. If it is not pure, it simply is not, for all that is not pure origin in itself is negation of this purity, and, therefore, of liberty. Since values impose a certain pressure, they would negate liberty. Similarly, if the action of God causes liberty to exist, it must make liberty be a being by another, which is the very negation of liberty.[1]

Contemporary Religious Philosophy of Liberty

One can show very simply that a particularly simple interpretation is at the base of Sartre's negations by calling upon other philosophies of existence, such as those of Gabriel Marcel or Louis Lavelle, and their interpretations of the same given, that is, human liberty.

First of all, instead of the simplified image of Sartre, they understand freedom in its authentic context of spiritual reality. Certainly freedom implies a certain independence or separation. However, freedom as it really exists appears primarily to be related to an encounter with value properly speaking, that is, with absolute value or good in itself. Value does not impose itself. It invites and calls one to accept and agree; but it leaves one perfectly free to consider this agreement or to refuse it. At the same time, value offers for one's consideration a choice as to how one should be himself. This should be precisely by responding to value, rather than to some

---

[1] See L.-B. Geiger, "Philosophie realiste et liberté," in *Philosophie et spiritualité* (Paris: Desclée, 1963), II, 35-59.

vulgar desire of satisfaction or possession, whether of power or pleasure.

This is a first liberation. However, it is completed only at the instant when one decides freely to make of himself, both by and for himself, an act of love and realization of the world of value, taken in its varying and hierarchical order. More fundamentally than a breaching or independance, understood in a purely negative sense, liberty of freedom presents itself to one's mind as a link, a response, and an assent. This is made to the value as value on the one hand, and, on the other, to that possibility within oneself by which he is able to respond to that value. It is as if one's innermost self made one recognize a dormant facility to materialize or to actuate that value in making it one's own by the free decision to henceforward will the good according to the truth.

At the same time, far from refusing any link whatsoever with any source which gives it being, freedom shows itself to be present in one by some Liberty or Act. While remaining distinct because Absolute, instead of remaining alien like some distinct cause, this freedom presents itself as that in which one continually participates to be and to be free.

Rather then efficient cause, the contemporary philosophers mentioned prefer to take recourse in the Platonic term: participation. However, they do not use it in the order between the objects of knowledge, that is, in an intelligible universe to be contemplated. Instead, they place it in the spiritual experience of one's activity, that is, on the side of the subject and not on that of the object. Thus, it expresses that experience, whose evidence was already expressed by the *Memoria* of St. Augustine and the latter's theme of "Deus intimior me meipso." This experience consists in an activity which is most authentically one's own, free, and thus, in a sense, most independent. At the same time it allows one to see most clearly that he is not it first source, but that it subsists in him from a source in which he lives, moves, and exists. This source is seen as conferring on one precisely that freedom which consists in a free response to the truth of the good as intuitively confronted, and as cleansed from the obscurities of instinct and its longings. Lavelle and Marcel do not hesitate to name this source God.

It remains necessary to discuss the difficult problem of values, specifically the question of their mode of being. If they are treated as the equivalent of things or even of Platonic Ideas, as if they were a gallery of pictures in a museum, then once again liberty runs the risk of falling back into a purely natural level of things.

It should be noted, however, that nobody, not even Sartre himself, has succeeded in realizing by the individual consciousness itself the total creation of his first step or leap and of his values. The "pour-soi," the consciousness or "néant" (nothing) rises up necessarily as a kind of obsession of the "en-soi" and leap ("projet") which is at the same time both free as the "pour-soi" and solid as the "en-soi." It is not a leap that one might choose or even invent. It is rather the absurd leap of nobody. It is the result of the absurd accident which is the birth of the "pour-soi." In order to avoid creation Sartre takes refuge in a kind of mythology.

Traditional philosophy is less extravagant in words, but more in agreement with reality, in defining liberty from the beginning as this mysterious agreement of oneself with a possibility which seems to come from within. This invites one to identify himself by choice with a possibility of oneself which does not itself depend for its being on one's choice.

A Christian Philosophy of Freedom

It is time now to draw some conclusions from these general ideas. It should be remembered, first of all, that one of the most difficult points in the religious conception of liberty is that same truth of creation which has appeared to converts from paganism to the Christian faith as the very sign of their liberation. On the contrary, to existential atheism as in general for a great number of philosophers, this truth appears as the very negation of liberty itself. This is so because it implies the dependence of creation on a cause, and hence on a being quite other than the creatures it causes to move and have their being. It seems to make one no more free than a remotely controlled machine. This then implies that the theme of liberty runs the risk of shutting off access to the sphere of religion for two distinct, but closely related reasons:

(1) the conception of liberty itself;
(2) the idea of our liberty being dependent upon the creative actions of God.

Let us briefly examine these points.

Concerning liberty itself, what is essential has already been stated. It is very important to present liberty under its true colors and to avoid simplifications. These may be useful for the imagination; but for many they impede rather than open the way to true liberty, since they imply a conception of liberty on a physical, rather than on a true spiritual basis. Such a message, far from constituting an invitation to growth and development in spiritual stature and to a certain and uninterrupted creation, appears as a promise of security bought at the price of higher aspirations.

However, the conception of liberty is not the only difficulty which confronts many contemporaries in reconciling their faith in liberty with the idea of God. It is indeed their idea of God and creative action that is equally involved. Here one touches upon the agonizing problems which all theologians know only too well, namely, the relationship of grace and liberty, physical promotion, divine concurrence, predestination, and human responsibility.

The intention here is not to take up again, even briefly, an exposé of the theological themes involved, but simply to make the following observation. Supposing one conceived for himself as exact a conception of one's true liberty as possible. One would confront almost insurmountable difficulties if he proceeded to place, either in front or outside of this liberty, a God who is its cause. Such a God would cause as the sun causes the warming of the atmosphere, or even as a living being of this universe begets another living being from which it is completely distinct and independent. Either one does not speak of God in relation to one's liberty and satisfies oneself by a phenomenological presentation of given human experiences, or one speaks of God. In the latter case, one must try, at least, to avoid those most egregious errors which, from their very nature, inevitably and irrevocably obscure the very data of the problem.

In this regard, one should call to mind the essential role that St. Thomas assigns to negative theology within the whole of theology. The words that open the treatise on the essence or the nature of God in the *Summa Theologica* itself should be taken quite seriously: "After having shown the existence of God, let us study the essence of God, that is to say, that which God is or rather that which he is not."[2] In the *Summa contra Gentiles*,[3] he observes that, in contrast to the knowledge of finite beings at which one arrives by the addition of positive differences, it is rather by a

[2] I, q. 3, prol.
[3] I, c. 14.

group of negations, made progressively more precise, that one attempts to discern the mystery of God. This is done without ever being able to obtain a positive grasp which, if had of the absolutely simple being, would necessarily be a direct vision of God himself.

If the affirmations of St. Thomas and of all the great theologians have any meaning, they say at least this: the word God designates a being whose fullness of being and perfection necessarily escapes the grasp of any created intellect. He is always incomprehensible, even for an intellect admitted by grace to the vision of God. Far from discouraging the spirit who loves God, this evidence of God's transcendence increases one's reverence and adoration, and the authenticity of one's love. Such is the condition of man's intelligence confronted with the word God; and he must never forget it. It must always be taken into account whenever one deals with a problem of anthropology or of ethics, and especially when one deals with the problem of freedom. This means that one must not work on the relation of freedom and of God without having realized the unique position that the word God occupies in the universe of one's mind.

Therefore, one cannot allow himself or his listeners to think that the freedom of man and God occupy in one sentence the same position as any subject or predicate. If God is the transcendent Being, the plenitude and source of all good and being, he cannot be exterior to anything in the univocal sense of spatial exteriority. He cannot be alien to anything or juxtaposed to anything, for he has no position. He is, on the contrary, interior to everything. More precisely, he is intimately present to everything that is, continually giving it true being. This is the presence that the theologians have taken so much trouble to specify. The very transcendence of God by which he is completely different from all that is finite implies his immanence, rather than opposing itself to it. The transcendence is not an infinite estrangement, which would terminate by coinciding with total absence and nothingness. It is rather the positive plenitude which necessarily comprises all perfection. By that very fact, it distinguishes itself from all finite being while at the same time being its permanent and superabundant source.

God cannot, therefore, be simply represented as something opposed to one's freedom, for this would imply an image which would lead to false perspectives. He is necessarily present as the very principle of one's freedom, not in order to limit or falsify it by his influence, but precisely to make it be: to give that authentic freedom of which one is aware. Certainly, it is impossible for one to think of his freedom and of God at the same time without danger of error. To deny it or to be astonished at it would be once again to forget that God transcends one's knowledge. Any philosopher or theologian, who would esteem himself capable of embracing God and his creatures in one perfect glance, would implicitly affirm that he is more than God. He would be the true super-God, judging and contemplating in one instant both God of whom he speaks and his works.

The first movement of freedom, then, will not be to revolt against God. Rather it will be to give thanks both that this gift is and that one finally knows that it is. The only way to be able to appreciate one's liberty, both as one's own and as rooted in an inexhaustible source, is precisely to understand that freedom as a free gift of oneself is a grace continually conferred on us by a source which is Gift by essence. A freedom which wishes only to be efficacy or will to power will seek above all to assert itself in opposing itself to anything. A liberty which understands itself as a free gift cannot but understand itself as participation in the Gift by essence, from which it is distinct, without being separated.

This less simplified conception of the relationship between one's freedom and its divine source permits one to avoid a great number of false problems relative to dependence upon the creative action of God. Certainly the mystery must remain if it is true that it could be clarified only if one clearly understood God and his relation to his work. But one can and must clearly say at least the following.

Freedom and Dependence

The notion of creation transcends efficient causality and places one once more in the field of analogy. To create is to make to be purely and simply, not to transform any preexistent material. A mechanic can construct a car which functions according to established laws and without his intervention to turn the pistons and wheels at each moment. Likewise, if an act is truly creative, it will posit true beings absolutely in the act of being and each will have the properties and nature demanded by its degree of being. Therefore, if God makes a freedom to be, the least one can say is that it is an authentic freedom which functions truly as freedom.

The continuous act, by which God gives freedom its being, will neither destroy it nor prevent it from being what it is and from functioning according to what it is, because it is precisely by that continuous gift that one's freedom is freedom. Such a dependence on its source results precisely in man's freedom being freedom: free in its being as well as in its act.

It remains true that the expression "efficient cause" or "creative cause" is suspect to many philosophers, Christian or not, because of the mechanical images that it inevitably suggests. Therefore, some have preferred to have recourse to other comparisons such as the relation which unites a work of art, a poem, or a piece of music to its author. Surely, the work depends on its author as an expression and a gift but not in a mechanical way. If in a certain sense the work is independent of the author and may continue to exist once the author has disappeared, it remains nevertheless the expression of his love of beauty which brought this work into being.

Other authors, such as Lavelle and Marcel, prefer the idea of participation. Be that as it may, the important point is not to believe that physical images are essential for the presentation of the notion of creation or the idea of the dependence of the creature upon God. This would make it more difficult, if not quite impossible, to reach Christian thought for minds sensible above all to the eminent dignity of our liberty and to the spiritual reality which it implies as its permanent principle. One should say the same for the notions of nature and substance. They may also imply images, which is correct and necessary. Nevertheless, these images make them liable to error in translating the realities of the spiritual order or of metaphysics.

Freedom and Law

There is an obstacle which one often creates for oneself without wishing it. This takes place when one is faced with the spiritual understanding of freedom, no longer under the aspect of dependence, but under that of the laws and norms. In doing this, one runs the risk of proposing God as a limit or an impediment against which one's freedom must inevitably stumble, and in which one's freedom finds an exterior limit which it can never surpass. This also is an image, and it is one which presents God first of all as in some way exterior to one's freedom. This image also presupposes that one's freedom should be without any other content than a gratuitous gesture: that it should be without law, without deliberation, without any other purpose than to show the will; that it should be no more than the absolute incoordination of gratuitous caprice.

However, far from being true freedom, this lack of coordination would be simply the physical or physiological decompression of energy, necessitated by its own pressure. This would remain in the domain of spontaneity, and in no way express that of freedom. True liberty appeals to and forms its own law. This is so in the same way in which a true scientist, in opposition to a dreamer, includes in the love of truth flowing from his spiritual spontaneity a rigorously demanding fidelity both to the object, which he tries to see correctly formed in his mind, and to the methods, which have proved their efficacy. To be truly free is not to be opposed to laws or values, but only to those laws and values forced upon one from outside and which one must fulfill out of fear of punishment or hope of gratification. This could never be the case where true freedom is face to face with good or with laws understood in their true essence.

For St. Thomas, however, all true law is finally founded on the natural law. This in turn is essentially nothing other than the tending towards good and end which was marked by God himself on every creature as the true expression of its nature. Freedom has no other law than to be free. But if it be a matter of the mind, and in no way of a fluctuating energy, then freedom implies in that wish to be free which is its law the wish to know the truth of the good toward which the whole action takes place.

In this light, the law of God does not appear as a barrier against which one necessarily sees the aspiration of his liberty destroyed. There is no extrinsic frontier to one's liberty and he can desire everything, the good and the evil. But good cannot do otherwise than to appear as that which ought to be, and evil as that which ought not to be. If one considers that as a barrier then it must be recognized that freedom indeed has its limits. Not to recognize these limits, or to be unable or unwilling to take account of them, is to be unable to act freely in the full sense of that word. It would be the same as making some blind gesture or one of whose worth one has no idea, and then resigning oneself bravely to the consequences. Under the pretext of a more pure freedom, the consequences would be produced without having dared to look the situation in face.

It is true that, at the same time, one both does and does not propose one's own law for oneself. As St. Augustine exclaims: who belongs more truly to oneself than oneself, and who is less one's own than oneself if one is what one is by another! Therefore, one must avoid relating freedom to law as a vital movement to a limit which operates from outside, or as a moving object which collides with an obstacle. Trees also are bound by certain limits, but it is in no way necessary to frame them with metal frames or to point out to them how large they must be or what shape they must assume, as one would do with blocks of cement. It is their own vital spontaneity which keeps them within their proper limits.

Finally, one must in no way conceive God as exercising external surveillance over one's actions in the same way in which parents either recompense or punish their children by watching whether or not they behave according to the rules set down. A God who would be obliged to spy on man in such a way, in order to assure the proper distribution of his sanctions according to man's good or evil behavior or according to the account man renders of himself, would be anything except God. It is well known how damaging to the mind of those who have realized the eminent dignity of the God-given free act is the presentation of a God-directed moral as a sanction, repentance, reparation, or merit added, so to speak, from outside to the proper value of the moral act.

Conclusion

To sum up, it can be said that the theme of human freedom meets religion in two perspectives: first, in its origin where it meets God as Creator, and, secondly, where freedom stands before God as lawgiver and judge. Freedom depends upon God for its very being; it must recognize him as its author and as the author of moral law.

On these two aspects, contemporary thought poses somewhat new problems which Christian philosophy must recognize. Most assuredly, the truth given to men by God must not be modified to the passing whim. On the other hand, one should be ready to recognize that there are some legitimate demands being made to give high value to the truth in the very manner in which one presents that truth. One must not confuse the truth with the more or less adequate expressions given to it, for by doing so one would risk confusing those expressions with truth itself and, consequently, falsifying the picture. One would then be like the pharisees who, by their blind fidelity to the letter, imposed heavy burdens on men's shoulders. Jesus himself declared it impossible to bear such burdens and wished in his love to remove them in order to liberate the human race.

In the same way, one must always be assiduous in freeing the true spirit of Christian philosophy from inadequate expressions and formulae. This is neither a desire to hide the truth nor a servile fear of wounding men's susceptibilities. Quite the contrary; it must be done in order to permit all facets of philosophy to be presented to one's contemporaries in a true and authentic form.

LOVE AND PERSONAL GROWTH

by

REVEREND ROBERT O. JOHANN, S.J.

The thesis of this paper can be stated quite simply. It is that love is the person's vocation. A person achieves himself and completes himself as a person only in the measure that he realizes love as a way of life. How this is so will be shown through a consideration of four related topics. First of all, love will be analyzed in terms of creative responsibility. Secondly, love will be considered as a way to the achievement of personal identity. Thirdly, an analysis of the structure of experience will disclose the role of love in the constitution of reality in its integrity. Finally, the relevance of Christian revelation to the achievement of a life of love will be sketched.

Love and Creative Responsibility

The word "responsibility" is employed in a variety of ways. Sometimes, for example, it is used as an equivalent for "duty" or "obligation." Thus one may describe an individual as "having a great many responsibilities." Again "responsibility" is often used in the sense of "self-determination." Responsibility, in this sense, is that for which young people today are more and more clamoring. What they are actually seeking is an ever greater freedom to determine for themselves the shape of their lives. Unfortunately, when used in this way, the idea of responsibility is all too often devoid of anything like genuine responsiveness. Responsiveness, however, is precisely the note on which I would like to concentrate. As used here, therefore, the word "responsibility" will designate that capacity in man to respond personally to the situation in which he finds himself, i.e., to act in a way proportionate to all the factors, values, and exigencies inherent in the situation.

In his little book, *Man's Place in Nature*, Max Scheler distinguishes man from the lower animals precisely in terms of his capacity to be genuinely responsive to his environment. Unlike man, the animal "lives, as it were, ecstatically immersed in its environment which it carries along as a snail carries its shell. It cannot transform the environment into an object."[1] The animal's actions are all reactions to stimuli as here and now affecting the present condition of the organism. For the animal, the environment does not exist in itself as objective or in its otherness, but only as impinging subjectively on its psycho-physical structure. With man, however, all this is changed. Man is precisely the being who has emerged or detached himself from nature and holds the disposition of his life in his own hands. For man, the environment begins to exist on its own terms. It becomes a world, acting upon man and calling for his personal answer. This answer is not automatic. It is something that man himself can shape and mold. By reason of his spirituality, man is able to appreciate the objective values and factors inherent in the situation and act accordingly. There exists, therefore, a certain interval between man as person and his environment. This interval is the necessary condition for freedom. Without it, the self would have no elbowroom, no possibility for reflection or choice. It would be a mere thing among things, wholly absorbed by the complex network of infra-human forces and no self at all. With it, however, man is able precisely to humanize his relationships with the world. In a word, he is able to step back, take a personal stand towards all that surrounds him, and, moreover, be responsible for the stand that he takes.

This native capacity which man has to give an original response to his environment, is one that stands in constant need of purification. There is, perhaps, no greater illusion than the idea that anyone, regardless of his past history or present dispositions, can be immediately and genuinely responsive to the real exigencies of his situation. This is an illusion that the long history of asceticism, that training ground for freedom, has constantly recognized. Responsiveness presupposes an openness to the other as other, and a willingness to let the other be itself. One cannot truly respond so long as one's life is commanded by prejudices inherited from the past or by present egoistic and self-centered desires. True responsibility, therefore, is something which demands discipline and train-

---

[1] Max Scheler, *Man's Place in Nature*, trans. by Hans Meyerhoff (New York: Noonday Press, 1961), p. 39.

ing. One has, indeed, to educate oneself for responsibility. It is such an education that St. Ignatius has in mind in the first two weeks of his *Spiritual Exercises,* of which the whole aim and direction is to help one achieve that inner freedom which is necessary if one is really to meet the demands of the situation. Their whole purpose is to enable one to be truly responsive to Him who is active in all encounters and who, in all answers to His actions, wills only that one deepen his union with Him and not remain in self-defeating isolation.

The idea that in his actions man is able to reply to the all-encompassing initiative of God Himself introduces the second notion indicated in the heading of this section—the notion, namely, of *creativity.* Precisely because the person encounters his environment within the horizon of the Infinite, he is never limited to what is merely matter-of-fact but is constantly passing beyond it. For man to experience anything as finite and determinate is for him to experience it, at the same time, as capable of indefinite improvement. His calling can therefore be said to be that of a perpetual renovator; he is a renewer by vocation. In the light of the possibilities which his presence to Being itself opens up to him, he is called upon constantly to be reshaping the face of the earth. Whatever is, falls short of what still might be. Man's role is to overcome this shortcoming, to exploit to the full the realm of possibility, to be constantly reworking the structures and determinations of the situation in which he finds himself so that they may become ever more adequate realizations of that full plenitude in which they participate and to which, as a person, he is open. For man, therefore, to be responsive to the Infinite in and through the finite is always and at the same time to be involved in a creative enterprise.

What then is the relationship between "creative responsibility" and "love"? They are, I think, one and the same. To undertake a life of creative responsibility is precisely to undertake a life of love. It is to embody in one's life all those qualities which philosophers of love have always associated with its very essence.

Thus, for example, Erich Fromm defines love in terms of four essential notes: *responsibility, knowledge, care,* and *respect.*[2] Obviously, these four notes are closely connected. Indeed, if responsibility is analyzed as in the preceding paragraphs, one can easily see how the three other qualities which Fromm adds to it are al-

[2] Erich Fromm, *The Art of Loving* (New York: Colophon Books, 1962), p. 26.

ready included within it. For, if responsibility is more than a matter of feeling responsible for others,[3] if it includes as an essential element the notion of responsiveness stressed above, then it is clear that responsibility cannot be had without knowledge. One can be responsive to a situation only insofar as he is thoroughly acquainted with the facts, exigencies, and possibilities of that situation. The same is true with the idea of care. One cannot respond to a situation in the sense of really meeting its needs and exploiting its possibilities unless he cares about it. Thus responsibility necessarily involves both knowing what is going on and being actively concerned with it. Finally, the fourth element, respect or reverence for the proper reality of the other, is likewise involved in the idea of genuine responsibility. An exercise of responsibility is, indeed, an exercise of one's ability to respond, to let one's actions in a particular situation be governed not by one's own whims or prejudices but precisely by the demands of the situation itself. It is to be attentive to the forces and factors actually functioning there and to act accordingly. It is, in short, a respect or reverence for the otherness of the other and a willingness to let the other function on his own terms. Thus it can be said that, if Fromm has been successful in his analysis of love, then the genuine meaning of love, discovered when one gets behind its sentimental façade, is identically the meaning which comes to the fore in a truly responsible life.

The same similarity of essential content can be found if our own analysis of creative responsibility is compared with the definition of love given by M. Nédoncelle. This philosopher defines love as a *volonté du promotion*.[4] He sees the loving person as one whose fundamental drive is directed to the enhancement of *the other*. To enhance or promote the being of the other is not for Nédoncelle a matter of making him over in one's own image. The true lover does not approach the other with a determinate plan for reshaping his life. What he wants is that the other grow and develop according to the inner exigencies of his own being. His aim is to co-operate as fully as possible in the other's realization of his own potential, for, as Nédoncelle sees it, personal life can only flower in a kind of inter-personal space. What the lover does, therefore, is to provide room for the other to grow in, that "root room" which he needs if he is to come to his full development as a person. Thus the

3 *Ibid.*, p. 28.
4 M. Nédoncelle, *Vers une philosophie de l'amour et de la personne* (Paris: Aubier, 1957), p. 15.

idea of promotion manages to combine in itself the two notions stressed above, that is, both the responsibility that one owes to others and the creativity that one can exercise in their regard.

Love, therefore, and creative responsibility are one and the same thing. Both, moreover, are beautifully united in the image which Heidegger uses to describe man's vocation. According to Heidegger, man's vocation is to be the Shepherd of Being. Now if one ignores Heidegger's scruples and identifies Being with God (as I would not hesitate to do), then one can say that man's ultimate calling is to be shepherd to his Lord, wholly intent on His full coming-to-presence, wholly bent on the realization of His kingdom, just as the shepherd is wholly concerned with the welfare of his flock. Man's fundamental vocation, in all his encounters, is to see to it that each of them become the occasion for a fuller realization of God's power and glory. For this is man's supreme dignity. He is able to hear, respond to, and love with all his heart, the One who is the Source of all. In so doing, he not only divinizes his own life but contributes to the fulfillment of God's life in time.

Love and Personal Identity

The notion of love as creative responsibility can have a helpful role to play in solving one of the hard problems with which educators are presently confronted: the problem of personal identity, of helping the individual to find his own proper place in the world.

In one sense, personal identity has always been a problem in human life, for man is a being who experiences himself as a *self,* as an entity that has emerged from the secure embrace of nature, and as one whose life has been placed in his own hands and to whom the future is necessarily a burden or a matter of decision. Man's relationships to his surroundings do not proceed automatically; he has to choose them and take a personal stand towards everything that is. His difficulty stems from the fact that he is not quite sure just what it is that is expected of him. Where can he look for guidance to know just what role he, as an individual, is supposed to play?

This has always been a problem for human consciousness. It is inevitably tied up with the gift of freedom, which is man's special prerogative. But if the problem has always been with man, there is no doubt that it has been rendered especially acute today. Although man's life has never unfolded with the sureness that characterizes brute nature, and although his relationships to his surroundings have never been determined simply by his natural instincts, still, up until now the individual always had outside help in determining the shape to be given his life. If merely natural patterns were never enough to guide him, he has, nevertheless, always found a measure of security in the social and institutional patterns that made up his human environment. Having emerged from *first nature*, the order of psycho-physical determinisms, he was newly embraced by a kind of *second nature*, the order of social habit. To a not inconsiderable extent, what was expected of him and the role he was supposed to play were mapped out beforehand by the societal framework in which he found himself. He was born into a settled way of life whose institutions and traditions contained answers to all the large questions so that the range of choices confronting his own freedom was relatively narrow. The big issue of his relationship to the world was already settled for him. Hence, all he had to busy himself about were the minor details.

This, however, is no longer the case. As one writer has put it, "the past has come unstuck." Due to a variety of factors—notably, contemporary man's increased sense of time and history, and the explosion that has taken place in the world of communications—institutional forms and frameworks no longer have the same authority as before. Man's profound awareness of temporal process has had the effect of relativizing many of the forms and patterns he once took to be absolute. What he once thought of as something set up by God, he now sees as something which man has achieved; and his confidence in it has been proportionately weakened. Moreover, there is also a tremendous range of alternative world views which contemporary communications have forced on the individual. Right from his infancy, he is literally bombarded by pluralism. Before the person is able to be formed and shaped within any single tradition, he is already forced to choose from among a whole host of them. Whereas traditional patterns were once able to provide the individual with a sense of the role he was supposed to play, all they do now is confuse him.

The result is that the individual is thrown back on himself and his own resources to a greater extent than ever before. There is only one thing of which he is sure. The past which has come unstuck cannot be put back together again. There is no returning to the non-questioning attitude of former times, for modern man recognizes that the security previously found in the acceptance of an established order was, to no little extent, a false one. He now sees that simple submission to patterns inherited from the past does little justice to the true dignity of the self. On the other hand, he is equally aware that the complete lack of a framework can lead only to chaos. So long as the individual is wholly on his own, he is lost. Thus, what modern man is desperately seeking is some kind of wholeness or order in which the individual can find a sense of direction and purpose, can feel himself at home, can satisfy his need to be a part of or participate in something larger than himself. Yet, this wholeness must be consistent with his freedom as a person and his right to continue to question all that mere man has achieved or may ever be able to achieve.

Now it is the contention of this paper that man can find the identity for which he is groping by recognizing and fulfilling his vocation to a life of creative responsibility. This is the third alternative confronting man and one which provides a way out of the dilemma that is presently torturing him. Man is not really forced, as he apparently thinks, to choose either a life of submission to some pre-established pattern in which he does not believe, or a life of lonely self-assertion and self-reliance in which there is nothing beyond himself to be counted on. Besides these two lives, by neither of which he can be truly satisfied, there is also the life of free co-operation with his Creator. It is not the case that he must either depend only on himself or lose himself in a world of man-made forms and patterns. Beyond the patterns, there is the pattern-less by excess. Beyond the realm of nature and of all the works of man, there is Being itself.

Man's true and ultimate identity which he is only now in a position to realize is precisely to be Being's agent, a lover of and a responder to Being. As such he will be wholly devoted to the task of bringing Being to an ever more full presence in the world, wholly committed to the work of continually renewing the face of the earth in the light of those possibilities which his very presence to Being opens to him. By giving himself to a life of service and co-operation with God, by recognizing and living his vocation as a promoter of Being, man will find himself lifted into a transcendent order which can provide sense and direction for his life.

Yet, this order, far from suppressing his freedom and personal initiative, will demand their continual exercise. It is much like what happens in a conversation between two people. A conversation is never a matter of mere self-assertion. It is precisely the position of oneself in relation to another, the position of a larger reality in which both participants are included. This inclusion, however, is not passive, but active. It does not do away with the freedom of either party but requires continuous initiative on both sides. A conversation is precisely an on-going work of co-operation, a conspiracy of freedoms. It is the position of an enveloping reality that heals each of the parties to it of his isolation and yet allows him to fully and freely be himself. The only requirement it places on freedom is that freedom have a focus, that it be responsibly oriented. The only demand is that each party really be attentive to the other, listen to what is being said, and make sure that his own remarks are relevant to the conversation and able to move it forward.

It is the same, though to an ever greater degree, in one's on-going dialogue with God. From one's life of responsiveness to Him, nothing at all is excluded; there is nothing extrinsic, nothing alien. In all daily encounters, it is precisely God Himself who addresses man and looks for his response. If one will but make his sole and overriding aim that of answering God in all that he does and of seeking continually to promote His fuller presence in the world, then not only will one find the identity for which he is looking and the cure for his loneliness, but he will also achieve the true meaning of his freedom which he is called to live to the hilt.

Love and Reality

The remarks made about personal identity in the preceding section can also throw important light upon the understanding of reality as a whole and of the demands that reality makes upon one. Reality is not something completely given or all spread out before one, of which one can become aware in its integrity from some point outside itself. Far from being a finished product, it is much more profoundly an on-going work in which one is involved. It is a still-to-be-accomplished task for which one is provided, ready-made as it were, only the raw materials. Let me explain what I mean.

Philosophers are notoriously concerned with the real as real, with reality in its integrity. All too often, however, they conceive of integral reality on the model of an organic structure or system. They tend to imagine it as a structured whole in which everything has its own determinate place, as a totality all of whose parts are functionally related to one another. What they forget, unfortunately, is that in such a conception man in his personhood and freedom is completely left out of account. To view the real as a whole in which everything is systematically related to everything else so as to form a single, encompassing structure, is to destroy both the selfhood of the self and the otherness of the other. In such a world-view there is no problem of personal identity. There are, indeed, no persons at all.

To think of the real as a whole in a way that is adequate to experience, one must take a different tack. Instead of seeing it as an organism or as a machine, the image to be employed is once again that of a conversation, of a dialogue, of an on-going encounter between each as a self and the whole range of the other. Its intelligibility belongs not to the order of logic but to the order of history and drama. It is a thoroughly temporal affair, full of the unpredictable. Constituted by the interaction of original powers, not all of whom are on friendly terms with one another, it is a process fraught with danger as well as promise. Reality involves conflict and collisions as well as happy outcomes, defeats as well as successes. The one thing certain is that what takes places does not predate its own accomplishment. Reality, therefore, is a still-to-be-finished story in which men themselves are the actors, and the story's ending will depend not only on the energy they bring to the task but on the way that energy is oriented.

This brings us back to our point. The way that reality as a whole discloses itself in experience and the shape that it assumes are not independent of one's own dispositions and the active contribution that one makes to it. Reality will make overall sense only insofar as one is concerned with what *is overall*. It will have ultimate meaning only insofar as one is himself open to the Ultimate, allows Him to come to presence in his life and, in the light of His presence, unifies all the diverse strands that confront one. If reality is to be more than a tale told by an idiot, it must be a tale of men's responsiveness to God, for the unity of the real is the unity of His all-consuming love. Only in the measure that men yield to this love and live by its light is reality itself equal to its own potential and its integrity finally achieved.

This thesis that the wholeness of reality is not a mere matter of fact but a matter of freedom, not something that is simply given but something that depends on men, has several important corollaries for educators. Let me simply indicate two of them. The first concerns the tendency in this age to separate knowledge and commitment. Knowledge and commitment are viewed as belonging to two completely different realms: knowledge belongs to the head and commitment to the heart. Moreover, a commitment, if it is to be a sound one, must be based on prior knowledge. In accordance with the scientific ideal of the times, one should proportion all commitments to the evidence already on hand to justify them. One should give himself to something only in the measure that such giving can be shown to be objectively warranted. Such, unfortunately, is all too frequently the attitude of young people today. They are not lacking in generosity, but they are hesitant. They sit back and want to be shown. They want the worth-whileness of a life of dedication to be demonstrated to them beforehand.

That this is impossible, however, follows immediately from what has been said. The meaning of life which love achieves cannot be had apart from love. As in the whole realm of the inter-personal, so also here, the general rule is: try it and see. This, of course, is not particularly helpful to minds torn by doubt. However, there is one further and important assistance that can be given them. One's own life can bear silent witness to the truth being affirmed. The worth-whileness of love, the wholeness it achieves, cannot be demonstrated by mere words, but it can be attested to by example, for a life of love has an eloquence of its own, a power to stir all who encounter it. In the measure that one, as he confronts his students, embodies in his own life the reality of which he speaks, an appeal will go out to them that is hard to resist, and they may be encouraged to take a first step.

The second corollary from what has been said concerns the goal of moral education. In an "open universe" such as has been described, moral training cannot be satisfied with inculcating a kind of conformism. It must look to the awakening of a true sense of creative and forward-looking responsibility. Right action is never simply the result of following rules; it cannot be prescribed in detail beforehand. Right action is precisely that which enhances the situation in which one finds oneself. But what genuinely enhances a situation cannot be known apart from a love which listens and is attentive to all the factors in the situation. Moral codes and lists of "don'ts" of course have their importance. They indicate factors that should always be taken into account and that one may not disregard. However, a list of things to be avoided will never indicate the positive action for which the situation calls. This can be discerned only by the eyes of love. Morality is a matter of meeting love's requirements. Therefore, only insofar as those receiving moral formation are educated along the lines of love, encouraged to exercise their own responsibility, and urged to leave the world better than they found it will they be truly educated as persons able to co-operate in God's own work of renewing the face of the earth.

Love and Revelation

In this final section I would like to touch briefly on the relationship between the above and the revelation which God has made of Himself in Christ and in His Church. There are people who, reading these remarks, might take them as a call to a kind of humanism that has little or nothing to do with revealed religion. At worst, they would argue that the structures and formalism of an institutionalized Church are actually repressive of the kind of creative responsibility that is being argued for here. At best, they would simply assert its irrelevance. "Man," they would say, "can fulfill the vocation you outline without aligning himself with any particular religious denomination." If he can do so, the implication is that he ought to.

Actually the case is quite different, for the doctrine of creative responsibility is not something that has been elaborated wholly apart from the Christian context with which it now must be brought into line. It has not emerged from an analysis of some neutral kind of experience from which Christ and His Church were absent. The experience of which it is a formulation is precisely the experience of a Christian, of one who has been nurtured from infancy towards a life of communion, and of one who is confident that the world makes ultimate sense because the Ultimate has not remained hidden but has revealed Himself and spoken to him through His Church— spoken, indeed, with accents of love. If Christians speak with assurance of God calling to us, it is because they have heard His voice, for the One from beyond the world has also entered into it. He is Emmanuel, God-with-us. The reason for His coming was to heal men's forgetfulness and to remind them of His love. The burden of His message is that men should love Him with all their hearts, and also love one another.

PART IV

DIALOGUES ON LOVE AND ON ECUMENISM

LOVE AND ETHICS

A ROUND-TABLE DISCUSSION

REVEREND ROBERT O. JOHANN, S.J., *Moderator*

NELS F. S. FERRÉ

REVEREND BERNARD HÄRING, C.SS.R.

VERY REVEREND REGINALD MASTERSON, O.P.

Report by REVEREND GEORGE F. MCLEAN, O.M.I.

A. THE MORAL RESPONSE[1]

by

REVEREND ROBERT O. JOHANN, S.J.

Morality is sometimes considered simply a matter of conformity. Because man never regards his actions as mere happenings but as deeds that are right or wrong, he is led to think that there must be a standard against which he can measure them and so determine their moral quality. The right action is the one conformed to the norm; the wrong action the one that deviates from it.

Although this idea is not false, it can easily be misunderstood. For it suggests that what a man ought to do, the course he ought to follow, is already completely spelled out; that there already exists a detailed recipe for righteousness; that a man has only to learn its directives and obey them.

Such a conception, I think, underlies the ambivalent attitude of many young people toward "traditional morality." On the one hand, they resent the idea of having to conform to a universal im-

1 This statement originally appeared in *America*, May 25, 1963.

135

personal code which seems to leave out of account their unique reality and initiative as persons and condemn them to a life not expressive of themselves. On the other, they need the assurance of being right that comes with doing the "accepted thing." They want to set out on their own but don't want to wind up alone.

Perhaps a way out of this crippling ambivalence is to view morality less as a matter of conformity than as one of responsiveness. This means that man is a moral being, not by himself or in relation to some impersonal ideal, but only in an interpersonal context, only as a person in relation to other persons. Our relationship to other persons is constitutive of our existence as persons.[2] It is only in communion with others that each of us can be himself. The achievement of communion, however, is never a settled fact. Consisting in a harmony of genuine liberties, it is essentially a continuous undertaking in which our very reality as persons involves us, and for whose maintenance and development we are singly and collectively responsible. Morality is grounded on the exigencies of this undertaking. To be moral, therefore, is not a matter of shaping one's life mechanically in accordance with some preconceived pattern. It is rather to be steadfastly heedful of the personal Other and genuinely responsive to the exigencies of communion in each situation facing us.

From this standpoint, both the value and limitations of a "code" approach to morality are readily seen. Since a code, to the extent it is valid, merely articulates abiding claims of the personal Other on my responsibility, conformity to a code is a help to meeting those claims. But it is only a help. A code is meant to illuminate my decisions, not make them for me. Submission to its injunctions can insure that factors permanently relevant to my practical decisions are taken into account. It cannot insure, however, that those decisions themselves will be wholly and adequately right. This is why, as the tradition has always insisted but we sometimes forget, a truly moral response is impossible without prudence. Only in the private light of prudence, which is the intellectual component of a personal, creative and loving responsiveness to the concrete and often conflicting demands of particular situations, can I adequately discern what here and now I ought to do.

Far, then, from stifling the individual conscience or the risks attendant on its exercise, a genuine morality is unthinkable with-

2 See my "Philosopher's Notebook," *ibid.*, Sept. 29, 1962.

out them. On the other hand, although it must forgo the comfortable security of mere conformity, it does not finally isolate me. For in the last analysis, morality is a matter of maintaining and deepening my union with You, "my first, fast, last friend," the One who ultimately addresses me in all the complex situations I confront. And my answer to You is moral if it is one of *discerning love*.

B. LOVE IN TRADITIONAL THOUGHT

by

VERY REVEREND REGINALD MASTERSON, O.P.

It has been said that when the expression of the Church in its cultural dimensions decays, there results for Catholics and Jews a certain ossification, and for Protestants, a certain evaporation. The oppressiveness of the purely legal approach in morality engenders a desire to move towards a more profound sense of personal responsibility, founding morality in the Christian sense on love. Yet, one is aware of the danger that in making this move the structures might somehow disappear. The problem is that of achieving a balance between these two points of view which will preserve what is valid in one approach and yet not lack the essential insights in the other.

The predominant question of these discussions has been that of resolving the tension which exists between the newly rediscovered dignity of the person and the fulfillment of this dignity within the context of society, or that of harmonizing personal fulfillment with communal obligation. This, of course, reflects a search for an ethical ideal. It is my intent to suggest from traditional ethics a way of resolving this tension and establishing a harmony between personal and communal growth by delineating the centrality of love in the traditional moral system.

The moral life, simply speaking, is a movement of the personality to the fullness of a life in God. Since it is a movement, it is obviously dynamic, and thus a process, growth, or actualization. In particular, this process is a way to the discovery of the Other. It would be possible to describe the God-ward movement in terms of panhedonism so that the growth to divine life remains egocentric in its emphasis. But though man cannot desire but to be happy and is right to see the way to God as the way to happiness, this is not the final word. The whole moral life must be animated by charity so that every act of virtue is an act of love and receives therefrom its specific orientation.

In this ideal there is no danger of loss of self-hood by an absorption in God; nor is there any danger of trying to subordinate the immensities of God to the demands of the ego. There is in man a double urge to give and receive. It is love which allows him to fuse these two contrary forces into one because where there is love, giving is itself a receiving. One is most fully himself when he most unreservedly gives himself to the Other. This is expressed in the Gospel phrase that one finds his life by losing it. In this way, self-realization ceases to be selfish when it discovers the true nature of love.

The traditional system constitutes a creative morality in which the self is enlarged and personality fulfilled through moral and intellectual life, through art, love and society, and especially through the shared life of God. In all of these creativities there is the tension of conflicts of duties. This is resolved by the fact that some beings have a greater claim to one's love than others. If love really suffuses the personality and directs human activity, then just as the tension between self-interested and disinterested love is resolved, other tensions can be resolved in the complete identity of will, begotten of love, between creature and Creator. This is both perfect obedience and perfect freedom; it is the freedom of the sons of God.

At the very core then of traditional teaching, there is the specifically Christian tension between dynamism and eschatology, that is, between, on the one hand, self fulfillment which includes the building of an earthly city or culture and the perfecting of one's natural powers in God's service and, on the other hand, the view of the God-ward journey in terms of the transitoriness of earthly culture. In theory as well as in practice, Christians have often evaded this tension by ranging themselves exclusively on the one side or the other, though there is truth on both sides. Self-fulfillment does include the building of an earthly culture and this is a work in which both Christian and non-Christian can join together. Man is to reach supernatural fullness through living the life of this earth, through the exercise and fulfillment of his natural powers. Thus, the supernatural includes a real natural end which, though essentially changed from the dynamism of an Aristotle, still involves purposes which can and should be acceptable to the non-Christian because they can be viewed in terms of the finite and earthly happiness of man and correspond to the root demands of human nature as such.

There remains, however, the apparently contradictory aspect of eschatological fulfillment in Christ. How can one be as though not using the world, and at the same time be concerned with the building of the temporal city? How can one fulfill the beatitude of Christ on the mount, "Blessed are the poor in spirit, for theirs is the kingdom of Heaven"? How can one in the words of the poet, "learn to care and not to care"? Again, the answer is found in love. This time it is in that God-given love of God by which man is put in immediate relationship to God and inspired with the spirit of detachment and disinterest in all his actions whether they be concerned with the inner life of the spirit or the affairs of the world. All man's energy is used in building up the temporal city since this is a part of man's cosmic return to God, but for that very reason the building is primarily an act of love for Him.

Finally, concerning the tension between the personal and the communal, the same conclusion is reached whether one proceeds from dynamism or eschatology, from the notion of the growth of person in a society, or from a purely other-worldly concentration on the figure of Christ. Man reaches the fullness of his stature by living a social life, for society is one of the factors which build up the total personality. The nation, the world, and the Mystical Body of Christ are communities of persons as a family is a community of persons. The family is built by the personal contribution of its members who, in turn, are fulfilled in the common life of the family. But because one's contribution is made in this earthly community, a member of the Mystical Body retains an element of reserve, not through lack of generosity, but through recognition that his world is still greater than these earthly dimensions.

It is apparent then that an identical conclusion is reached whether one begins in terms of personal fulfillment or communal life. The consideration of human society in terms of personal fulfillment and happiness leads to extensive involvement in the affairs of the everyday world, loving its beauty and laboring to heal its wounds. The consideration, necessary for a Christian, of human society in terms of the Mystical Body of Christ enriches the concept of duty to one's neighbor in terms not merely of this world but of the next. The material of charity and love remains the life and things of this world; their validity is not destroyed. The Christian uses and loves them, and knows that they can be of other-worldly significance. It is such wholehearted love which is the key to personal and social harmonization, to the realization of a social ideal.

C. AGAPE: NEW TESTAMENT LOVE

by

NELS F. S. FERRÉ

Our age of rapid transition and cultural fluidity needs a theology which, while reliable, is also open-ended and flexible. Agape, the New Testament kind of love, is the determinative and distinctive motif of the Christian faith.[1] Here Agape means not a philosophical principle, but the Incarnate Word: God's *Self* revelation in Christ as a kind of life, or personal Spirit.

A Christian moment is one that cannot be generalized into a philosophic principle alone, because it is a personal communication where the message is the Messenger. Christ, the Christian moment, however, is also a Socratic occasion in the sense that Chalcedon is normative psychology, for only in Jesus Christ, the Love of God made Flesh, does one fully understand human nature and man's rightful relation to God. Ethically the Sermon on the Mount, Romans 12, and I Cor. 13 seem normative for the Christian faith, all of which are overwhelmingly based on Agape. Agape is the God-centered, Christ-centered Love, which is outgoing, inclusive and unconditional.

It is necessary to distinguish Agape from other kinds of love: eros, which is self-centered, desiring love; and *philia,* which is the

[1] Martin D'arcy, *The Mind and Heart of Love* (New York: Holt, 1947); Bernard Häring, *The Law of Christ,* tr. by E. Kaiser (Westminster, Md.: Newman, 1961), 3 vols.; James Moffatt, *The Moffatt New Testament Commentary* (New York: Harper); A. Nygren, *Agape and Eros,* tr. by P. Watson (Philadelphia: Westminster, 1953); Viktor Warnach, *Agape* (Düsseldorf: Patmos-Verlag, 1951).

mutual, covenant, conditional love. God gives us eros and the possibility for *philia*, but in the last analysis neither of them is possible until one understands the Agape of God. One must go his own way in order to become a real, genuine being but he cannot fulfill that way until he finds the Love of God as it is in Christ.

Agape, furthermore, synthesizes the subjective and the objective, the good and the right. Sir David Ross, in his Gifford Lectures, *The Good and Right*, defines the good as dispositional or intentional and the right as a matter of the concrete consequences that flow from any action. Now, insofar as one takes Agape as the standard of ethics, it is necessary to accept this good because it comes from God and is God. But one cannot possibly be good unless he is at the same time completely and concretely concerned with the objective situation and the people themselves who are involved. Thus, to be good, one is under divine obligation to study all that is necessary to act in a situation and to follow his informed intention with the best possible concrete act. Since the good involves the right, moreover, which ultimately is a matter of both the individual and the community, Agape can never be personal without being communal. Agape demands full and complete stress on both the individual and his integrity and upon the community.

Agape, again, cannot be falsely other-worldly because the more one genuinely worships the God who is the Creator of the world, the more one must be concretely and completely concerned with his ethical responsibilities. Since He who is the Creator is completely concerned with His creatures, to be children of God and belong to the Divine Community involves accepting responsibility for the world. In this sense there can be no real dichotomy between the sacred and the secular.

Finally, Agape cannot possibly be fanatical and moralistic, even though it is completely concerned with both the devotional and the social life and its responsibilities. There can be no false tutelage because when one is concerned with the community while an individual or group needs to be left alone, it is a part of Agape to do just that. At the same time when there is need for the exercise of responsibility this is done more deftly, more completely and more absolutely in the Agape and the Holy Spirit. By Agape, one is more open, flexible, understanding and cooperative. In it there can be no fanaticism or legalism.

God has commanded absolute love of Himself and absolute love of His neighbor. Love is made the law because that commandment cannot be kept as law. Nevertheless, though law becomes bankrupt as law, if there is realized that love which fulfills the law nothing is taken away from the law. By grace and a new relationship of freedom, we find that love which cannot ignore structures, regulations, and responsibilities. This inner demand becomes the fundamental note in ethics and enables one to fulfill his obligations. God has commanded absolute love in order that the law which cannot be kept as law might be fulfilled as love.

D. LOVE AND MORALITY

by

Reverend Bernard Häring, C.SS.R.

In summarizing the meaning of the primacy of love, it is difficult to understand it as uniting subjectivity and objectivity if they first have been disassociated, for it is artificial to conceive an objective world without love. The greatest objectivity and the one which supports the whole world is that inter-personal relation which is the life of the triune God. The whole of His life is inter-personal, each of the Three Persons existing totally related to the other. Rather than one person first existing and then relating by love subjectively to the other, all three exist in their mutual love. Our world, insofar as it comes from God and is objective in this most profound sense, recalls to us the glory and splendor of the love of God. If one makes something objective and doesn't find there the claim, values, message, and order of love, how can he, as a human being, unite them?

This problem might be illustrated by discussions within the Council on marriage and the family. For some theologians, marriage is an institution with the objective goals of procreation, education, and mutual help, to which might be added the subjective goal of conjugal love. However, texts from the first book of the

Holy Scripture manifest with what tremendous love God conceived and executed this plan of creating two persons for one another, who by finding one another receive the order to be creative. Procreation and education is not only a goal or an economic or objective order without love. It is still more the very goal, the very finalization of conjugal love. Only in loving one another as persons can parents also love their children, not only as an economic goal, but as persons. It is this total view that constitutes marriage as the sacramental image of the covenant of love between Christ and the Church. Where this love is strong, it is procreative, creative, and fruitful for the whole Church.

So it is in all things. If one first found an objective order and did not find there the love of God, he would have found nothing. Because God is love, if He creates, He creates in love, and the whole creation through its real order brings the message of His love. Therefore, an objective philosophy and theology must first see this personal order. Behind all things is the Triune Personal God. All things carry his message to persons who exist through His call of love. This can be more deeply appreciated if seen in the light of the Incarnate Word of the Father, of whom St. Thomas says so profoundly "Non est Verbum qualicumque sed est Verbum spirans amorem." It is not an ordinary word but one which breathes the love of the Holy Spirit.

A philosophy or an ethics which first establishes duties and commandments that are imposed and only then annexes the motive is not objective. It leaves a separation between the subject and the object. It is not inter-personal and is without the dialogue by which the loving God brings us the message of His love. An ethics of values is a great help in seeing the objective order of love. There is no anarchy there, for where God's love has been creative, His wisdom has established an order of values which should be a message, an image, and an appeal of this tremendous love. In that appeal of love, one finds the depth of the objective order; the subjectivity which attempts to unite them with love is human and right. Men unite things with their love because they bear love in themselves and their order in the world is love. Objectivity is the message of a person, the loving God, and therefore always the message of love.

Finally, another example, can be taken from the 8th commandment: Thou shalt not lie. One who offends his neighbor by his statements, even if he can prove that what he says did happen, is a liar in the deepest sense of the Bible. Genuine truth is present when there is the image of the Word of God, who is not only a word, but the Word that breathes love. Therefore, one speaks the truth in the theological sense when he brings loving truth, the message of the loving God who is truth and gives us the truth of salvation.

This relation of truth and love has appeared in the deliberations of the Vatican Council concerning the sources of revelation. A minority within the Catholic Church considered tradition first as a collection of concepts or things to be believed, conserved, and possibly used as weapons against other schools. But the real insight of the increasingly great majority of the Council is that truth or tradition is a torrent of the revealed life of the loving God which can be grasped only insofar as one is in love. The message of love is the truth of salvation. This implies the Johannine approach, that where there is unselfish love there God is operating in man and the doors are open to the real world of love. Love is not something which is annexed to reality or which has to unite impersonal objectivity.

One cannot fulfill or even understand any commandment if he does not see that it is a message of love. The sinner takes commandments as limits opposed to his freedom. But if he is once renewed in his mind and reborn through the working of the Holy Spirit he finds in all things the message of love. Far from seeing the law as a limit opposed to his freedom, he not only does not transgress the law but he prefers it. Love is a commandment for the reborn son of God, for the renewed heart. The law of love cannot be imposed through threatening; it can be fulfilled only in accordance with the measure of the grace or love Christ has given. Where a person feels the urge of this love of Christ, he no longer discusses with God whether something is imposed under pain of sin. Rather, he feels that he is freed into the love of God and that he would lose his renewed existence or way of life if he were to refuse an invitation of the love of God. The son of Adam is provoked by the law to its transgression and cannot understand that there is a higher and totally different law of the Spirit who gives life in Christ Jesus. Law is not as the sinner sees it; it is a tremendous power that frees and assures the fulfillment of what is totally a calling of love.

E. DISCUSSION

I. Love: Natural and Supernatural

II. Love and Norm

III. Love and Ends in Marriage

IV. Love and Structure in Ethics

I. Love: Natural and Supernatural

Father Häring: In considering the relation between the ultimate ground of love and freedom and between natural love and the specific kind of divine and redeemed love, it is essential to remember that God is love and that for this reason the cross comes before creation. Before God created the world, He meant to make men free and to have them go their own way in order that they might become genuine beings and develop a genuine community. On this level God works indirectly through the grace that is in nature. It is very important to recognize this grace or love operating in nature and preparing for the full consummation of the direct and inclusive love of God as seen in Christ. Hence, there is a conscience which is contextual with regard to the community of the particular stage in human history and which must be obeyed because this is the only level of present attainment.

Since all such ways of developing selfhood and community are preparatory to the sole understanding of God in Christ where He comes as the inclusive, creative, and open love, that love of conscience is also secondary and merely preparatory. Thus, it too is to be judged, corrected, and transformed by the fuller love of God when conscience, which is the human side, is related to the image of God. Christ is concretely, visibly, and declaratively this God. The image of God is then not the power of creation, reason, or law, because God is neither reason nor judge, but Love! Therefore, the fundamental image of God is the concrete manifestation of love in Christ as the Incarnation. When this is seen we can enter into that community which is the very meaning and consummation of life. The two kinds of love come together in freedom because man has metaphysical freedom in order to arrive at spiritual freedom. He has the freedom of contrary choice in order to find the freedom in which he says: I want to do Thy will and love Thy will; Thy duty has become my song in the night.

II. Love and Norm

Father Johann: It is only love that puts us in the presence of the other and it is only through love that we can be responsive to the other. But since the panel has granted this primacy of love and the necessity of determining one's life in terms of the exigencies of love, I would like to play the part of the Devil's Advocate and ask how one goes about discerning these exigencies. For one humbly working his way towards this position of a more adequate appreciation of love, there are still difficulties as to how the individual forms his own conscience.

What does he consult; how does he regard various positions with which he finds himself confronted and which sometimes seem to go against what he believes to be the exigencies of love? Is there in any sense in this particular context for the role of nature as it has been traditionally understood in terms of structure? Does structure in this context play the same role as it played before? Are the structures of human nature final and finished or are they open to modification? Can love be creative as regards nature, as well? Having made love one's goal, how does one decide what love means and what is right in these concrete circumstances? Is one to be guided simply by some individual illumination or is there something objective? If so, does one then go back to the same positions as the past or does love, as the overall motive, imply a different basis for the appreciation of what is required?

Father Masterson: In the Old Law man's response to nature had to be commanded because he lacked the full freedom of the sons of God; he needed detailed prescriptions because he lacked an inner connaturality of love to the objectivity which he found about him. With the transformation of the interior man through grace there came a more spontaneous response of love. This is above all an unwritten law, and it might be said that love does not need a law. The husband who must sit down and decide what he must do in order to please his wife, in a sense, has lost the sense of love. Furthermore, there is a new found freedom of things that are of supererogation and which love seeks out without being required.

The notion of councils, in the New Testament rather than in the Old, implies that love seeks to pour forth itself completely in a connatural love.

Secondarily the law of love does require objectivation insofar, for example, as certain things must be fulfilled in the reception of the sacraments: the opening to new grace, to a greater sharing in Christ's life, and to a new love. Furthermore, certain things must be stated contrary or not contrary to this love, for, while nature is transformed, St. Paul notes the existence of a constant warfare. Though one enjoys the freedom of the sons of God, there is a painful working out of this conformity of one's love to His love, of one's will to His will, and of one's peace in the depths of His peace. Hence, the law of love or of Agape is written in the hearts of men through their sharing in the life of grace and charity, but it is this loving response to God's order in nature which secondarily requires some rectification. This allows for tremendous freedom as regards what one must do or not do.

Dr. Ferré: Objective reality is the Holy Spirit, and a supernatural relationship of grace apart from which one cannot have the requisite action. The Holy Spirit, however, is corporate or communal in nature; he is, in fact, the soul of the Church. Therefore there can be no right action that is not within the Church. It can be shown practically that the community is prerequisite for moral action; and because it is of the Holy Spirit, it is defined as an open, universal, concerned, creative community. God, as creative being, motivates this community of action.

It is necessary to have rules as directives for a community. This is true in a family, in a university, and similarly in our well structured Church. These rules and regulations are not ultimate and can lead to a form of legalism if divorced from right intention and treated inflexibly without attention to the persons involved. Nevertheless directives are necessary and it is part of love to become submissive to such rules and regulations as are for the common good. Rules are needed, but they themselves must be motivated by love, found in love, and state the truth in love.

Father Häring: St. Augustine's "Love and do what you will" must be understood as: have love and do what true, genuine love wishes. Love would be absent or at least very inefficacious and imperfect if it did not find the right order by connaturality. In fact, rules, and indoctrination would not help one determine the right act in the present circumstances if one did not have this internal connaturality of love which is the gratuitous gift of the Holy Spirit.

Love does not transgress the law, and as a sinner one finds necessary protection of his love in the laws of the Church. But there is a great danger that one who does not see that the very heart of the matter is love might follow (worst of all) situational ethics—that of keeping a small tradition or secondary rule and transgressing or destroying the great order of love. That is a sign that one is not permeated with divine love or a living faith. If one has love he listens to the message of God and finds that all things urge him to keep the great order of love.

Man needs the Church because he is still a sinner and the Church is the revelation of the rallying call of Christ. But one must not consider the Church first as an objective institution, a lawgiver proclaiming her own positive and changing law, and only secondarily as proclaiming the Gospel and invoking the Holy Spirit. One of the chief points of the Vatican Council's Constitution on the Church is that she is to be considered above all as a spouse of Christ, a community of love by the power of the Holy Spirit and through the blood of our Redeemer. Hence all the laws of the Church must be tested anew in every century and in great humility by the Church to see if, for these men and this culture, they are still expressive of their own mystery of love. On their part, Christians who wish to know the real and objective order must consider the whole Church and not merely the first approach to some small points of law.

If one wishes to know what is really good as a way of life, he must above all look to Christ and to all His words. Beyond this one must find the image of Christ in the saints of the Church and in such humble and faithful personalities as Pope John. One would never understand even the inspired book of Holy Scripture if he did not look upon men who in these time are, by the Holy Spirit, living in adoring and redeeming love. Through them one finds the deepest message of love in Holy Scripture.

III. Love and Ends in Marriage

Dr. Grisez: It would seem that one cannot speak of conjugal love without speaking of the goods of marriage: procreation, mutual help, and the remedy of concupiscence. While reproduction without love is beastiality, conjugal love that is not one of the three goods mentioned, or all of them, is meaningless. It is true that conjugal love, besides being natural, is also charity; but charity in the form of conjugal love receives its direction and specification from these three goods. If one introduces a false dichotomy between these traditionally mentioned goods of marriage and conjugal love, then the latter must always predominate. But if such a dichotomy is avoided, it would be much more accurate and much less misleading to say that procreation, mutual love, and the remedy of concupiscence are the goods which discriminate and guide actions rather than to say that this is done by conjugal love.

Father Häring: It is quite evident that parental love is an essential specification of conjugal love and that this must be integrated with charity or Agape, because otherwise it is never purified. The question concerns the way in which these are integrated. It would not be normal for a couple to enter marriage in order to have children now, saying that they wish to love one another later on. They get married because they love one another and wish to love one another and to grow in this love. They know that in marriage this means joining the creative love of God, and the more they love one another the more they wish the fecundity of their love. If they do not love one another, their marriage will not fulfill the three goods mentioned. For example, if they exploit one another in the framework of modern culture, they will not desire children or at least not more than one for their personal fulfillment.

In order to integrate love and the goals of marriage, marriage must be seen as a sacrament representing the covenant of an adoring and redeeming love. Hence married love is right if it gives glory to God and if it redeems or frees the other from selfishness. A marriage represents the covenant between Christ and the Church, which is a covenant of infinite fecundity. But it does so only through the love of Christ, as it is only through that love that the Church becomes the mother of all living. Just so the Church has her fecundity through the Gospel and not through a law that she first imposes. If a married couple does not love one another deeply and unselfishly, no external forms can convince them to have many children. They would not have the strength and the insight. First they must love one another as persons and know that theirs is a specific love according to which they love one another in the service of life.

The approach should not be from the goals as commands concerning things that must be done, but from the connaturality of an Agape or a love that comes from God and constitutes a deep unity with one's spouse. This love leads to the desire to help one another and to find numberless expressions of conjugal love, which in turn is a remedy which induces a desire for children and helps in their education. Such an approach is concerned with the very essence of conjugal love, whose natural ordination to its primary goal is neither in economic terms nor imposed from without. The primary ordination, which is of the very nature of the sacrament which is a covenant of love and hence already integrated with love, is a fecundity not only in this world but for eternal life.

These considerations alone do not resolve all cases. The couples themselves must study the love of God which is manifested first in the intensity of their love for one another, the depth of their faith, and the strength of the hope for eternal life. They study their means in food, housing, etc., because these are gifts of the loving God and they must return this according to the measure of the talents they have received. This is a responsibility; but in the Christian mind responsibility is generosity. One receives the freedom as sharer of God's love, and by this connaturality he can evaluate the present opportunities for the different way in which God leads men.

Dr. Ferré: One might wonder concerning the extent to which romantic love in the western, so-called Christian, sense is a necessity for marriage. In Asia some of the best marriages were between people who had not seen each other before they were married. This raises the question of whether there be structures of nature which are important and which God began on the level of nature. Perhaps one underestimates God's way of working if he does not also begin, in one sense, on this level, though one must not end there.

Successful marriage might also be considered a matter of moral equals under God and of common responsibility as well as common Gospel. I do not believe that children are a necessary part of family life because a marriage is had where two are together under God; and indeed, some cannot have children. God as a creator chooses His creations freely and responsibly, and morally responsible families are morally responsible for choosing their children. Under certain circumstances having fourteen children may not be better than having two or five. One can love five children with all one's heart and one's love would not be greater if he had fourteen. As a matter of fact, it may be quite irresponsible and manifest a lack of love to let nature take its course rather than exercise morally responsible choice in freedom under God. Here, as a Protestant and with the population explosion threatening the whole world, I advocate the responsible use of the freedom, responsibility and love which God has given us.

IV. Love and Structure in Ethics

Father Johann: There is a recent emphasis on God as love and on reality as being fundamentally inter-personal and achieved in communion which has not been sufficiently attended to in past moral treatises. Such treatises and their particular elaboration of natural law are founded on what might be called a substantialist metaphysics or a metaphysics of individual substances, which is perhaps not the most adequate way to conceive human reality. In moral life it orients persons toward conforming their actions to a code with less concern for doing the right thing in the particular situation than retaining the more comfortable position of not having broken some rule.

In the place of this it is not sufficient to appeal to love and hope love will be the light. To say that it must be a discerning love simply urges the question of how love discerns these exigencies. To refer to the specific nature of conjugal love raises the issue of how and where one identifies this specific nature of conjugal love. Is it from one's own experience of love, from someone's description of the nature of man, or from the idea of the nature of community? Without dropping the notion of natural law it might be suggested that one interpret nature, in this case, as the nature not of an individual man but of the inter-personal, of a community which constantly has to be achieved. This would express the full nature of man and allow for the identification of exigencies which transcend oneself and are both prescriptive and objective. Such a reinterpretation of what is meant by objective structure would be less an abandonment of tradition for Sartrean existentialism, than the recognition of the primacy of love expressed by Christ in the Gospel.

Dr. Ferré: On the question of whether there are structures in nature which are presupposed by, or directive of, love it should be emphasized that human nature is social or communal. Man is both a self and a *socius*. Agape implies that the community must allow the greatest possible development, freedom, responsibility, and maturity for each individual and group; whereas each individual must be responsibly concerned about the community. The building of both a freedom and a faithfulness in fellowship is the very essence of human nature itself, which cannot be satisfied apart from an open community. Hence, the love of God is required by the law of nature.

Man's life with others by its very nature is both precarious and predictable. One can neither plan fully and become self-sufficient and self-satisfied, nor fail to accept the kind of predictability which is there. God has balanced precariousness and predictability in such a way that one must support such structures as families, communities, citizens, and nations. If this responsibility is not faced now man will destroy the world. Though it is often said that man is now free from nature, he has never been more dependent upon it. Hence, love must take into consideration the technological development of man.

This leads beyond man's requirement of nature and his situation as a technological creature to the kind of fulfilling community which can be found in the Church and in Christ. In Him there is neither male nor female, neither Jew nor Greek, because all are one. Hence nature itself must be understood in terms of history; history in terms of the Church as a community; the Church in terms of Christ; and Christ in terms of the sovereign love Who created the world, within Whose meaning we exist, and apart from Whom we can never find fulfillment.

Father Häring: If one considers the nature of man in a totally individualistic way, he has only one problem: the salvation of his own soul. Such total self-centeredness even in the way of salvation would doubtfully be the supernatural way of Christ and would need to be strongly compensated by conformity to rules as a protection against anarchy.

In contrast the biblical understanding of man as the image of God is centered on an inter-personal relationship. Man's deepest meaning is to be called by the Triune God as a loving person, to hear this appeal through his neighbor, and to become himself by delivering himself into the arms of God through his neighbor. In this understanding man is not in such great danger of breaking the order of love because his final question of conscience is always whether something builds up the community of pure love.

In this, one must be aware of the complexity of the historical order. There is always interference from the old Adam's self-centered nature, and from the spirits of darkness working in the world. If man is totally a sinner and the world, even after the coming of Christ, is more under the power of the devil than of Christ, then men must be rigorously subjected to mechanical law. But the greatest reality in our world is neither the first Adam nor the devil, but the powerful love of Christ. Though man is still sinner, he feels a need for this love; and though the kingdom of God is not yet fulfilled, there is the powerful presence of the love of Christ working through the Holy Spirit within the Church and within those who open themselves in faith. If one trusts himself to this life he begins to realize how long his road of conversion may still be and how great his need for purification. Then by the power of the love of Christ he can humbly accept the necessity of rules, of responsibility, and of denying himself for the needs of community, for he then trusts more in the liberating power of the Gospel and of the Holy Spirit than in outward laws. It is a question of accent: who is first, Christ or the devil; and what is first in one's faith, acting by the Holy Spirit or the working out of Adam?

Father Masterson: This entire movement toward a new morality is an attempt to turn away from a false legalism and fundamentalism in order to move towards the center. It is traditional Catholic teaching that the law of Christ is an inward law, in relation to which the outward is secondary. In practice there has been too much emphasis on the law as outward fulfillment. To move towards the reality of Christ as an inward law and freedom is not to create a vacuum, but to develop a new love-filled attitude toward the law, which will always remain to rectify and norm right love. The process of renewal is difficult, but the Church is being renewed in this inward spirit of Christ's love, freedom, and respect for law.

PHILOSOPHICAL ISSUES IN ECUMENISM

A PANEL DISCUSSION

REVEREND GEORGE F. McLEAN, O.M.I., *Moderator*

REVEREND AVERY DULLES, S.J.

NELS F. S. FERRÉ

Report by REVEREND GEORGE F. McLEAN, O.M.I.

A. PHILOSOPHY AND CHRISTIAN FAITH

by

NELS F. S. FERRÉ

The Roman Church obviously has an official, though not a revealed, philosophy and it is important to distinguish carefully between the two. Protestantism has none, as its whole history indicates; any attempt to settle a philosophy on Protestantism is doomed to failure. It is possible, however, to make a good case that Luther was not entirely a nominalist, though he was certainly very much influenced by nominalism. Despite what he says against reason, he had some very distinct philosophical presuppositions. There are four possible positions with regard to the relation between philosophy and theology.[1] The Church has an official philosophy. The strength of this position is obviously its provision of universality for discussion and permanence of position. Regardless of one's own attitude towards it, it provides a definite stance in terms of which people can speak to one another. Obviously, Thomas Aquinas created a great synthesis and all have

---

[1] Nels F.S. Ferré, *Reason in Religion* (Edinburgh: Nelson, 1963).

every right to use him in their different ways. The weaknesses of this position are the tendency towards rigidity and the danger of becoming outmoded with the passage of time. It would be a rationalization to attempt to make St. Thomas into, for example, the first Christian existentialist. His statement that "esse est actus purus" is made in a spirit and context different from the contemporary existentialism stemming from Kirkegaard.

A second possibility would be that the Christian Church use no philosophy. This is held by those who believe that biblical theology and biblical orthodoxy are ultimate. In the middle of the 17th century, biblical theology struggled to free itself from scholasticism both within and outside the Catholic Church. Barthianism espouses this "no philosophy" position very strongly today. The strength of this position lies in the definiteness which revelation provides. Thus, Billy Graham can simply say: "The Bible says" and there is no question of philosophy. Its weaknesses lie in the fact that, without being conscious of it, a theology might use some present philosophy uncritically as a vehicle which would ultimately distort, truncate, or dilute the Christian faith, which might thereafter become ossified within it. It is very interesting to observe some who hold that one must not use philosophies, now eagerly using linguistic analysis to prove by philosophy that they are right.

The third position would have the Christian faith carry on a constant creative dialogue with contemporary philosophy. This approach avoids the Protestant tendency to reduce the faith to the question of justification. However, if Christian faith conceives of philosophy as in any way dealing with truth, even with ultimate truth, and if the Christian faith then claims to be true at its center, theology is necessarily ontology and cannot use alien forms of ontology such as those of being, process, or non-being without denying its own truth and becoming self-contradictory. If God can be interpreted or even proved by some other reality outside of God, then God is not the ultimate truth but Himself referred to some other categories of reality.

The fourth position would recognize God according to the main definitions of God in the New Testament, as spirit, as love, yes, as the Personal Spirit who is Agape. If these definitions of God are correct and if Christ is the truth, then a Christian theology is also philosophy in the sense that it sheds the most complete possible light on experience. This is not a popular position within Protestant circles. Theologically or doctrinally there is no ultimate perspective, nevertheless, that can more fully inform Christian doctrine than that God is Agape, and philosophically this position can illuminate truth as can no other ultimate category. Problems for Christians in philosophy are due mostly to a false framework for the picture of Christ or the Incarnation. The world is rejecting the Christian faith because of the framework and not because of the picture. This framework must be corrected in order to allow the truth to shine through. Such was my experience, for instance, in explaining many points to Buddhists in Japan.

Whereas, it might be supposed that truth for truth's sake would be a more complete philosophical position, the Christian believes that ultimate reality is best known through God's love. The Christian claim is reflected as well in the Buddhist legend that when Buddha received his enlightenment and could have entered into Nirvana he was concerned not with truth for truth's sake but with truth for humanity's sake, for which reason he renounced his own deliverance.

It is also thought that Christians believe in God ultimately as a personality, whereas God is not a spiritual personality but a personal Spirit. If personality be defined: "a complete substance subsisting of itself and separate from all else" (*Summa Theologica,* III, q. 16, a. 12, ad 2) one cannot possibly believe in the Incarnation because this would then imply the existence of two Gods, not to mention the Holy Spirit. On the other hand, if God is not ultimately personality but personal Spirit, spirit becomes the ultimate category of identity. Then God can become Incarnate because the Spirit has this capacity to work in nature and history and to remain self-same; and at the same time He can be with His creation and communicate with that which is not Himself.

Non-being is the most important category for the Buddhist; but one could not be a Christian if he did not believe in non-being. God is creative being, and non-being is a presupposition for creation. Since Hindus believe that each experience is fragmentary, insufficient, and illusory they have to come to a category of the substantive self. Because Buddhism believes that each moment of experience is fraught with suffering and illusion it escapes into a non-being, a non-self, as the ultimate category. Christians do not have to hold either position, because they hold that the self is potentiality in process. This necessarily involves non-being, for since

God could not and would not create if everything already was, creation involves non-being.

The use, as ultimate, of Aristotle's category of substance (that which requires only itself in order to exist) creates all the illegitimate problems of Christian philosophy concerning God's relation to the world. For instance Tillich says that it is impossible to believe in *a* God or in *the* God or in a personal living God. By definition God is infinite. But such a God cannot be outside the world because then he would be related to the world and hence no longer absolute or unconditioned. Therefore, he avers, there can be no transcendent realm or being, there can only be transcendent meaning. Because similarly, there can be nothing infinite within history or creation, one can no longer believe in God, and atheism or *a*-theism in this sense is a philosophical necessity. If one begins with a doctrine of being, analytically Tillich is right. I believe, however, that this whole approach is mistaken. The problem is not with the doctrine of God in the Christian faith, but with the fact that we have accepted the Greek kind of metaphysics which makes this doctrine impossible.

Other examples may be found in suffering and change. God is not supposed to be able to suffer because the perfect cannot suffer. But that the perfect cannot suffer is based on a definition of being, not on a definition of the God of Jesus Christ who is concerned. Love can and does suffer. God is not supposed to be able to change either because he is perfect in substance; but that kind of ultimate is not Christian. If God is ultimate love, it is not a limitation but a perfection for God to have relations. The very perfection of God is to create and generosity is his nature. Therefore, to create that to which one relates and to be related in a perfect redeeming relation is the very nature of God as ultimate. For God to change is not a contradiction, because He who is the most changeless is the most changeful. He who is the most changeless love as Spirit, nevertheless, relates Himself to each individual, and each makes a difference to God. God is not self-sufficient being; He is self-sufficient Love.

Process philosophy, however better, is no substitution. Taken ultimately existentialism has its great truth, but is not a Christian option. In Protestant circles some now are going over to the process philosophy of Whitehead and others as a substitute, and to some extent this thought can be accommodated. But fundamentally process philosophy states that there is no ultimate being, God being as much created as creating; that the thoughts create the thinker; that the thoughts, that is, everything, are inter-related and completely interdependent; and that all inter-relations are finite and in process. Such an appraisal constitutes a perfect definition of the heart of Buddhist philosophy and in itself is inadequate.

The point of departure is essential. Being provides no adequate doctrine of becoming, becoming or process no adequate doctrine of being; non-being no adequate doctrine of either. However, if one begins with God himself as the personal Spirit who is love, rather than with substance philosophy or philosophy of being or of process, he will be able to solve all these problems. God as creative being, as love, and as spirit in New Testament categories is the point of departure for an adequate doctrine of what is permanent, of what becomes, and of non-being as the presupposition for creativity. A revolution in Christian philosophy will take place, but it cannot begin until man can with his head, as well as his heart, believe that Christ is the Truth.

B. PHILOSOPHY: CATHOLIC AND PROTESTANT

by

REVEREND AVERY DULLES, S.J.

My interest in philosophy has been continuous and, as in the case of Dr. Ferré, so much involved with my interest in religion, in Christianity, and in theology that I have never been able to separate the two interests. My own progress toward faith was always accompanied by a strong attraction to the great philosopher-theologians of the Middle Ages, such as Augustine and Aquinas. It is difficult to limit their Christian wisdom and synthesis to either philosophy or theology, for their thought is sufficiently comprehensive to include both.

The ecumenical dialogue of these past 20 years has concentrated very much on such areas as ecclesiology and the sacraments. There has been a lack of discussion directly on philosophy as an ecumenical issue, though this area has great potentialities.

Just as there is a Christian philosophy, there is certainly such a thing as a Catholic philosophy. The First Vatican Council, by its statements on the competence of unaided human reason in the sphere of moral and religious knowledge, made this clear. The *de facto* existence of Catholic philosophy is fairly evident from the theses commonly taught in Catholic schools of philosophy regarding, for example, the existence and nature of God, including his infinity and immutability, creation and its freedom, God's sovereign happiness and lack of suffering, his providence over all things, his establishment of laws of nature, and man's constitution out of matter and a soul which is spiritual and immortal. These can be termed Catholic philosophical positions. While Thomism is approved as a safe philosophical system, it can in no way be called, in an exclusive sense, the Catholic philosophy.

Furthermore, the Vatican Council made it clear that Catholics are committed to the distinction of the two orders: the natural and the supernatural, reason and faith, philosophy and theology. To some extent these orders undoubtedly overlap. The theologian on the basis of the data of faith can ask certain questions which the philosopher can ask on the basis of reason and experience, and hence there will be an overlap in their conclusions and a mutual influence between philosophy and theology in the man who is both a Catholic and a philosopher.

Catholic philosophy is philosophy operating under the guidance of revelation, which is recognized as being a necessary influence in order for philosophy to attain its own proper perfection. This evokes an analogy with the notion of grace perfecting nature: just as grace restores and perfects nature which has been somewhat weakened due to original sin, so theology restores and perfects philosophy, which would otherwise err, and enables the philosopher to attain properly philosophical insights, which he could not attain without the help of revelation and theology. There are many ways of conceiving the positive relationship of Catholic philosophy to faith. It serves both as preamble to faith and as a sort of instrument in the service of faith and theology.

There does not appear to be such a thing as a Protestant philosophy. Gilson gives some reasons for this in his *Christianity and Philosophy*. As far as orthodox Protestantism is concerned, he calls attention to the doctrine of the total corruption of human nature through original sin, which excludes any sort of philosophically virtuous exercise of human reason outside of faith. In this connection he adduces some negative quotations from Luther concerning philosophy. Since Calvin's approval was of a Christian philosophy worked out on the basis of revelation rather than of natural reason, he too did not approve philosophy as an independent discipline. Barth's invitation to philosophers to acknowledge their discipline as profane and godless is in a sense more Lutheran than Calvinistic.

In practice many Protestants deny most of the Catholic philosophical theses outlined above. Such positions as the knowability by reason alone of God and His attributes, the analogy of being, and the idea of natural law are characteristically denied by most Protestant theologians. There has, however, been a very notable resurgence of philosophy of religion within Protestantism, which is largely based on a phenomenology of religious experience. Certainly since the time of Schleiermacher and the 19th-century liberals, very distinguished Protestant contributions have been made to the philosophy of religion. However, this would not constitute a metaphysics or ontology as the term is commonly understood.

The question of how much philosophical issues have contributed to the division between Protestants and Catholics demands special historical study. However, one might refer to the interesting book of Louis Bouyer, *The Spirit and Forms of Protestantism*, which stresses the importance of nominalism. It is the position of that work that the basic new religious insights of Luther, Calvin and other reformers could have been formulated in an orthodox way, but that the prevalence of nominalistic philosophy at the time disoriented these insights and led them into the radical denials responsible for the separation. Many analogies can be drawn between nominalist philosophy and the original Protestant positions, especially those of Luther, who nevertheless was not a pure nominalist. The twofold predestination to salvation and damnation, fiducial faith, the denial of tradition as a source of doctrine, substitutionary atonement on the part of Christ, merely forensic justification—i.e., a purely extrinsic declaration by God that a man is just without working an interior transformation: all these could be related to the tenets of nominalist philosophy and probably should be. However, there is no pure correspondence between nominalism and Protestantism, as Calvin's formation seems to have been more Scotistic and other reformers were more Thomistic, while there were Catholics who were nominalists.

In recent centuries the differences have perhaps been accentuated, since Protestant philosophies have tended to be subjective, evolutionist, and activistic, as opposed to Catholic thinking which has been increasingly objectivist and metaphysicist, emphasizing the truth of conceptual knowledge. The differences were hardened as Catholicism became more static, at least during the 17th, 18th and 19th centuries. Mutual understanding by the different philosophical traditions of the various confessions has become increasingly difficult.

To speak in terms of reunion would be too optimistic at the present time, but it is possible at least to work in that direction, perhaps, by a better use of philosophy. What then can philosophy do to contribute to the progressive improvement of mutual understanding? The first thing would be to clarify and carefully note the points of philosophical difference. The positions in philosophy to which a man is committed as a Catholic should be clearly understood even though that may involve an initial difficulty. No fruitful dialogue can take place unless founded on an understanding of where one stands to begin with. Catholicism would seem to be wedded to a metaphysical realism, i.e., to the view that human abstract concepts can have value and be predicated without any falsification even of God. The whole movement of Catholic dogma has been away from the non-metaphysical, and only implicitly ontological, biblical manner of statement to the great definitions of faith which took place beginning with the 4th century. In taking up the dogmatic form of utterance and accepting the legitimacy of a dogmatic transposition of the Christian message, the Church seems to have committed itself to a basic metaphysical realism. John Courtney Murray in his *The Problem of God* observes, "I do not think that the first ecumenical question is what think ye of the Church? or even, what think ye of Christ? The dialogue would rise out of the current confusion, if the first question raised were what think ye of the Nicene homousion."[2] Until this issue is squarely faced the dialogue will be confused.

Further, in order that the dialogue be fruitful, there must be some possibility of progress. This might consist in a better understanding of one's own philosophical positions by explaining them more coherently to each other, and in assimilating what one can

---

2 John C. Murray, *The Problem of God, Yesterday and Today* (New Haven: Yale Univ. Press, 1964), p. 53.

of the true insights of the other position. In gradually restating one's positions in an effort to meet the criticism developed by the other confession, one can expand the area of mutual communication. Often Catholics misunderstand Protestant philosophical positions, thinking that Protestants, by their denial of metaphysics and natural theology, are necessarily committed to a total agnosticism in which man can have no real or meaningful contact with God. Similarly, Protestants often misconceive Catholicism as a pure rationalism which holds that purely human and natural concepts can be applied without any kind of correction to God, thus reducing God to the position of one being among many.

A better understanding of the classical doctrine of analogy implying the negative theology—the *via negationis et eminentiae*—can contribute greatly to a rapprochement. For instance in his book on Karl Barth,[3] Bouillard notes certain resemblances between the dialectic of analogical discourse and the dialectic of "dialectical theology." The new trends in personalistic philosophy are also something which seem to cut across confessional lines. Catholic philosophy has been notably invigorated by a recognition that the properly personal is a privileged starting point for true philosophical and theological knowledge. The current accent on inter-personal knowledge and on the type of intuitive thinking which this involves has tended to relieve us of the exaggerated emphasis on the concept and on objectivity in thought into which Catholicism fell during the polemics of the counter-Reformation.

C. DISCUSSION

I. Philosophy and Faith

II. Creation and Divine Immutability

III. Personalism

I. Philosophy and Faith

Dr. Ferré: The assumption that Protestantism cannot have a philosophy because it considers original sin to have so destroyed the

[3] Henri Bouillard, *Karl Barth* (Paris: Aubier, 1957).

image of God in man that he can no longer think objectively would be true only of one part of Protestantism. As is evidenced by his book on Anselm,[4] even Karl Barth has a philosophy in the sense of taking the Christ-event as central to truth and seeing by the eyes of faith, that is, in terms of supernatural grace by which the distorting tensions of sin are overcome. Man's tendency to rationalize is eliminated by the power of forgiveness which overcomes man's drives to self-justification. There is considerable agreement in recognizing that natural man and natural theology are only capable of an understanding of God that is negative. Man the sinner is threatened at the center of his being by revelation, not by this kind of natural theology. There is, of course, a relation between finitude and sin because finitude prevents full and true seeing. But if neither total doubt nor total seeing, i.e., neither seeing nothing at all nor seeing as God sees, is possible for man, then the question is rather one of the extent to which any positive seeing is possible. The sinner tends to self-justification, self-protection, or self-promotion; he tends to rationalize. The saint, on the other hand, being freed by the power of the Holy Spirit, is able to see truth even when it convicts him and is against him. Thus, there is a relation between grace and truth in philosophy that cannot be avoided, no matter what the specific Church to which one belongs.

It is obviously true that there are strong elements of nominalism in Luther, but their extent has recently been debated and the question is not settled. In more recent times the Hegelian movement, and in the present situation men like Brand Blanshard with objective idealism, or the whole personalist movement for that matter, are not at all in the nominalistic tradition. On the Roman Catholic side existentialism is not foreign today though quite different from earlier orientations. Therefore on both sides—and there has never been a time when men have been so unencumbered by defensiveness and so open to genuine search—the philosophic positions can converge. Metaphysical realism is a difficult problem. Modern man, in any case, is in a different position from Aristotle and Aquinas because he understands that man does not live in a special creation of 6,000 years ago but in a cosmological process in which the history of creation and the pedagogical process are not yet complete. This situation with regard to the history of creation presents three choices. One might hold that what came first must

---

[4] Karl Barth, *Anselm: Fides quaerens intellectum* (London: SCM, 1960).

somehow account for what came afterwards; but such a position amounts to a reductionistic naturalism. Or, one might hold that the fullest possible account for the process now at hand gives us the truth; but why should any human being make this moment of time the standard for ultimate truth no matter how distant in time? Finally, the third or eschatological position has difficulties because the evidence is not yet in and confronts, besides, such facts as evil and sin. If one takes this impasse seriously he finds himself in a situation in which he must make an ultimate faith judgment; he must live by faith. Having made one's judgment, in faith one can take Christ or revelation as central and formulate a philosophy.

It is, indeed, completely impossible in the present situation to have a philosophy with no presuppositions of any kind. Every being other than God has a presupposition, a stance which he cannot prove. One cannot prove God, for this would have to be done from something more real than God. God is what one proves by, not what one proves! Any metaphysical realism must acknowledge that behind every metaphysics there is a faith judgment; that even one's reason, so to speak, must be justified.

Being as such, as the basis for analogy, will never make it possible for one to come to God. What is required, as says Barth, is an *analogia Christi* rather than an *analogia entis*. That is, one must work not from the average or general data of experience but from the highest revelation of God in terms of both analogy and paradox: analogy in the sense that one does not know God as He is in Himself, and paradox lest one make man's own process, or continuity, or knowledge the ultimate standard. It should be emphasized that man's knowledge of God is true; Incarnation is man's best basis for understanding both God and the world. But man does not gaze upon the eternity and the fullness of God. He is unworthy of this and will be revealed to him as God wills.

One must be a personalist in one sense, of course, if by that one means belief in a personal God who knows and cares. However, it would be erroneous to consider the ultimate to be personality rather than personal Spirit. Incarnation would be impossible if God were the cosmic Self. God is the ultimate Self and there can be only one God. I believe, however, that there is no hope for Christian philosophy unless it holds to the Nicean position that the very nature of God has come into human history. If God has not become incarnate, there is no ultimate standard for theology or for philosophy.

Working with the New Testament and the early Church and insisting upon the extension of the Incarnation one can develop a real theology, philosophy and psychology. Unfortunately the true humanity of Christ and the true humanity of creation have been somehow or other separated. The New Testament teaches that the law came through Moses, but grace and truth came through Jesus Christ and of His fullness we all have received, grace for grace, until one be filled with the fullness of God. In Him the fullness of God dwells bodily, and in Him one is made full until all come to the nature of the stature of the fullness of Christ. These are the eloquent statements to the effect that Christ shows men not only who God is but who they are. To say that Chalcedon is normative psychology is not to reduce theology to psychology, but to lift psychology into the reality of theology. Here one sees that man cannot be real and fulfilled until he is rightly related to God; and this is realized only in so far as he meets God in encounter. Because He is Personal Spirit Christ is both transcendent and literally in men (*Christus pro nobis et in nobis*). In this fact lies the full doctrine of the relation of philosophy to theology.

Father Dulles: The idea of God coming to men in revelation, shattering their categories, and making them judge themselves is an interesting one. The concept of philosophy mentioned would seem to be largely a reflection upon revelation rather than something which, at least in theory, could be prior to the reception of revelation. A thought process which takes its starting point from the revelation of the self-giving God as Spirit pouring Himself out in Agape or charity, as manifested in the New Testament, certainly affords an otherwise unattainable insight into the nature of God and of ourselves.

Nevertheless, in order to get ultimate intelligibility into a thing like love, it would have to be understood in terms of being. Since to say that God is love is at least to say that God *is* love and that God's love *is*, its understanding—to the extent that love can be philosophically understood at all—would involve grasping love as a mode of being. One would be rightly concerned about any reduction of everything to a kind of general, vague, or average concept of being as a common denominator, for this would demean God. However, the meaning of analogy is that being is not said in the same sense of, for example, this table and of God, but a sense which is simply diverse (*simpliciter diversus*). Hence, in anything one says about God the difference from any creature is greater than the similitude. If one has a rich and flexible concept of being it would seem absolutely necessary to speak to God as the source of all being, for God is eminent and ultimate being. Further, if one does have this rich notion of being which is irreducible to a concept, then God is being, love is being, and act is being, for otherwise they would be nothing. Thus for the philosophical understanding being has a certain primacy over the other categories.

However, for an existential Christian understanding, categories such as love may be more meaningful, in the sense of being more readily reducible to experience and having more vitality in transforming one's existence and being better able to be proclaimed. Possibly we are too rigid in insisting on the primacy of being, even though it will have to be the governing notion in a fully systematic philosophy. In any case God should not be defined in terms of being, nor should being be defined in terms of God, since being and God cannot be defined but only confusedly grasped by the human intellect.

Dr. Ferré: Certainly if being means is-ness it must be accepted as a category along with the category of becoming and of non-being. But God is not to be defined in terms of being (God is being); rather, being is to be defined in terms of God. Being itself is an intellectual abstraction which one does not meet; but one can meet God in Jesus Christ, one does meet love. What most fully makes God really understandable to me is not a category of being but that God is love and that He creates. Hence, it would be better not to redefine being as a separate category, but in using it as a way of talking about the is-ness, to note that this is-ness is that of His love and of His creating.

If being is defined in terms of love then love is the more fecund and seminal category, in the sense that now love also can explain non-being, which is the infinite created power of God. God can create because it is the nature of Deity always to exceed in possibility any and every actuality. Therefore the very meaning of non-being is explained in terms of the generosity which is the love by which God can create. It is the same with becoming and all the categories. Hence, it is not a question of denying the category of being in its place and as defining the is-ness, but the category of ultimacy I think belongs to the New Testament categories even philosophically.

To say that being cannot be related without becoming limited is the effect of studying these problems from the point of view of being as an abstraction rather than from that God as love.

II. Creation and Divine Immutability

Dr. Ferré: If God is creative and if something new is coming to be, then this can be only by a generosity on the part of God which implies potentiality by which God as love is related to the world. To deny potentiality to God would make him a substantive actuality according to a doctrine of being. The Greek philosophers began with such a notion of being; but a better way of talking about being, is to speak of it in terms of God rather than of God in terms of being. To come to a genuine, creative, ecumenical movement in which Catholics and Protestants really try to meet one another, it may be that both will have to re-think what is secondary and press forward toward the very center of their faith to find categories that are real and in terms of which both can come together. Throughout the world the lack of active interest in the Church manifests that the Christian faith is in danger of collapse from within, both from the lack of spiritual power to solve the problems of war and race and from the need to rethink in more creative terms an historical philosophical tradition which is not necessary to the Christian faith.

Mother Clarke: Augustine is recognized by all as having put love in the center of philosophy and as having been led to his greatest insights through living out his love. Nevertheless, in the beginning of the *Confessions* and in other works he gives even more attention to the explanation of God as immutability than does St. Thomas. In many places, for example in the *De Trinitate,* he says that God is the supreme and infinite being because He is immutable. He would seem to make immutability the most distinctive characteristic of God.

Dr. Ferré: In considering why Augustine, who in his understanding of God and of life stressed love so fundamentally, also emphasized immutability as the almost central nature of God, it would be inadequate simply to trace this back to the neo-Platonic circle of his thinking. Furthermore, it would be most unfortunate to understand this immutability as implying that there is nothing in God that can become involved, that God is not one who knows and cares, or that he is removed and known only by intermediaries as in the *Timaeus* of Plato.

Augustine did have a keen sense of time which underlined the fact that everything is passing away while God alone remains. More particularly, it would seem that a spiritual, theological, and devotional understanding of God's immutability would be based on the faithfulness of his eternal nature whereby He is completely dependable, not only by will but by nature.

It is true that in eternity God cannot suffer, if suffering be understood as a negation of the eternal nature and purpose of God, or of his victorious and sovereign love. But the Christian faith holds that God becomes incarnate and involved in history, and that as such he suffers in the Son. It is not possible, however, to dichotomize God as though the Father is there and the Son here with no co-inherence. These are ways of, so to speak, analyzing God, but the understanding of those things in God must be simultaneously true because of his nature. In this sense God, who is the most changeless, is the one who relates Himself in some way.

With an operational understanding of God it is possible to appreciate that God is present in the table in a different way from that in which he is present in the saint, as indicated by the words: where two or three are gathered together, I will be in their midst. In a table or in a gunman God is present impersonally as the directing, sustaining, creational entity, that is, through operative rather than cooperative grace as he is in a saint.

This distinction is reflected in the difference between the Old Testament's referring mostly to the Spirit of God and the New Testament mostly to Holy Spirit. There the Spirit of God would refer to the preparatory presence of God in conscience and human conduct apart from Christ or apart from the fullness of his understanding and grace. Such an understanding would allow for the ultimate immutability, steadfastness, and dependability of God and his sovereign victory over creation. At the same time it would allow him to be the God of Love, of creation, and of the cross, who participates, cares, and becomes involved.

It may be possible to consider a doctrine of absolute being which has no real connection with creation. In this sense creation would not be from this being but would be somehow or other accidental, external, or fortuitous. However, if creation is from God's very nature, love, and generosity, then there is something in God which needs to create, not out of deficiency but out of fullness. There would be something in God by which he needs to relate Himself to His children, not because He is imperfect but because He is perfect. Thus, the less good a mother is the more she can abandon her children, while the more perfect a mother is the more she needs the perfection of motherhood. This is a need for children in the sense, not of dependence, but of the perfection of motherhood. In a similar way, the perfection of God's love in creation is not that of having no relations, but that of being in relation. Hence it would seem preferable to abandon a pagan doctrine of being that has been smuggled into the Roman Catholic Church and the whole of Western civilization and been deified, and to go on creatively, particularly within the Church, toward the Christian understanding of philosophy.

Father Dulles: Non-being is simply a being of reason—that is, a way of conceiving what really is not as though it were, without implying that it really is. Thus, in terms of God as the Absolute Being, the non-existence of relative being is quite conceivable and the whole notion of creation, which comes from God's love, is to "make be" a relative being where relative being was not or did not have to be. Hence, being and non-being are categories in terms of which one can think of creation.

It is relatively easy to arrive at God in terms of *actus purus* and *ipsum esse subsistens,* but it is much more difficult to combine this with the biblical data concerning the God who cares for man, is concerned, and involves Himself in history through the various comings of his grace and the Incarnation whereby he actually becomes man. The question is whether it is satisfactory to say that God has not really related Himself to man, but that this "coming" is just a relation of reason in God? Certainly it would not involve a real growth of God in the sense of adding some accretion to God's being in a way that would imply that He had not been perfect before, but was perfectible and growing. This would reduce God to the status of a limited being alongside of the rest, and constitute a form of atheism which would be just as contrary to faith as a remote God. Hence, the problem is one of understanding God as genuinely absolute and infinite and as totally responsible for all outside of Himself, while in some mysterious way being concerned. This would seem to demand something of an intentional aspect which would not prejudice the infinity and essential immutability of God as affirmed by faith.

III. Personalism

Dr. Ferré: If spirit is the identity of unity and if God is the one spirit of unity in reality, literally men are one if they are in the spirit. But since all are distinct as personalities, they are at the same time from or of God, and for or to God as the ultimate category of reality. With spirit as the category of unity and the personal as the category of distinctness, it is possible to have a real doctrine of Incarnation. The doctrine of the Trinity which has been developed by the Roman Catholic Church is actually the best prototype for a philosophy because in the doctrine of the Trinity there is perfect coherence and distinctness. These two characterize all reality, which fundamentally is one because it is from God by creation, while the history of the world is a pedagogical process whereby God makes us distinct. The important thing is to learn to become genuine individuals by the pedagogical process in which one learns to live love. Christ is the center of this learning process because in Him one sees what to learn, that is, who God, the final lesson, is. This is a unity which never destroys the distinctness. Hence, in eternity there will be distinctness; but it will be accompanied by the perfection of spirit which is the resting and being in God.

Mother Clarke: It might be well to distinguish between two types of personalistic philosophies. One would be the philosophy of personalism which is characteristic of certain American groups such as those in California and at Boston University, of which Brightman is an exponent and outstanding innovator. It was much more from this point of view that in his synthesis Teilhard de Chardin considered spirit to be really present in some diminished manner in all things, even the most insignificant. Thus, considering things outside of man would mean limiting what is real.

Dr. Ferré: Being itself does not exist anywhere; it is an abstraction in people's minds. Hence, it does not seem best to have a philosophy of being starting with such an abstraction. What does exist is God, persons, creation, and relations; being is best defined in terms of God and the Augustinian point of view of the Trinity of the Persons.

There are many types of personalism, such as that of Mounier, Brightman, and others. That of Brightman is very dangerous because it became connected with idealism. Hence it would not allow the traditional notion of creation but reduced creation to the consciousness of God organized in one peculiar way for a particular purpose. This does not allow a distinct reality for creation as a pedagogical medium. Furthermore, since this kind of personalism is one of personality in a limited sense rather than of spirit, even though Brightman uses a spiritual category, it does not allow for incarnation. On the other hand, an Augustinian type of personalism would be acceptable if it emphasized both spirit and love, as well as the personal. Since one cannot have love that is not personal or spirit that is not ultimately guided by and informed by the personal, such a personalism would affirm all three categories in their right relationship.

INDEX OF NAMES

173